Fernando Pessoa

PHILOSOPHICAL OUTSIDERS

Philip Kitcher and Anjan Chakravartty, Series Editors

*

Philosophical Outsiders explores philosophical contributions made by influential thinkers well known for their work beyond the orthodox philosophical canon, including those who have advanced the sciences, political or social thought, or the arts and humanities. Through engagement with philosophical reflection in works usually viewed in a different light, this series aims to expand and diversify the canon itself, and to initiate wide-ranging conversations between philosophy and other traditions of inquiry.

*

Toni Morrison: Imagining Freedom
Lawrie Balfour

George Orwell: The Ethics of Equality
Peter Brian Barry

Fernando Pessoa: Imagination and the Self
Jonardon Ganeri

Fernando Pessoa

Imagination and the Self

JONARDON GANERI

OXFORD
UNIVERSITY PRESS

OXFORD
UNIVERSITY PRESS

Oxford University Press is a department of the University of Oxford. It furthers the University's objective of excellence in research, scholarship, and education by publishing worldwide. Oxford is a registered trade mark of Oxford University Press in the UK and certain other countries.

Published in the United States of America by Oxford University Press
198 Madison Avenue, New York, NY 10016, United States of America.

Library of Congress Cataloging-in-Publication Data
Names: Ganeri, Jonardon, author.
Title: Fernando Pessoa : imagination and the self / Jonardon Ganeri.
Description: New York, NY, United States of America :
Oxford University Press, [2024] | Series: Philosophical outsiders |
Includes bibliographical references.
Identifiers: LCCN 2024012743 (print) | LCCN 2024012744 (ebook) |
ISBN 9780197636688 (hardback) | ISBN 9780197636701 (epub)
Subjects: LCSH: Identity (Philosophical concept) | Self (Philosophy) |
Pessoa, Fernando, 1888–1935—Philosophy. | Pessoa, Fernando,
1888–1935—Criticism and interpretation. |
Philosophy, Portuguese—20th century.
Classification: LCC BD236 .G36 2024 (print) | LCC BD236 (ebook) |
DDC 126—dc23/eng/20240325
LC record available at https://lccn.loc.gov/2024012743
LC ebook record available at https://lccn.loc.gov/2024012744

DOI: 10.1093/oso/9780197636688.001.0001

Printed by Integrated Books International, United States of America

MIX
Paper
FSC FSC® C183721

Contents

Acknowledgements vii

Introduction 1

PART I POETS AND PLURALS

1. Be Plural! A Poet's Creed 11
   Keats: The Poet as Chameleon 11
   Shakespeare: The Protean Poet 13
   Pessoa: The Poet of Immersion 16

2. Self-Estrangement 24
   In the Forest of Estrangement 24
   "Something Obscure in the Centre of My Being" 26
   Imagining Being Another 32

PART II VARIETIES OF HETERONYMOUS EXPERIENCE

3. Artefact Minds 41
   Simulacron-3 41
   Avatars and *Avatāras* 48

4. A Life Lived in Serial, and in Parallel 55
   Rudra and the Makropulos Case 55
   One Life Lived in Parallel? 63
   Death as Deletion 68

PART III MAKE-BELIEVE AND THE *MOKṢOPĀYA*

5. Reality++ 77
Vasiṣṭha's Argument 78
Realism Retrieved 82

6. Names Used Twice Over 94
Second Līlā 94
Imagining Seeing Yourself 100
A Common Ground? 103

PART IV PESSOA'S IMAGINARY INDIA

7. Pessoa in India 109
Imagining India 109
An "Indian Ideal" 113
Pessoa and the Upaniṣads 118
Pessoa's Indian Peers 122

8. "One Intellectual Breeze" 125
Cosmic Consciousness: Whitman, Carpenter 125
Is the Cosmos Conscious? Coleridge, James 135
A Pessoan Cosmopsychism 141

Glossary 147
Bibliography 151
Index 159

Acknowledgements

I am very grateful to Philip Kitcher and Anjan Chakravartty for their kind invitation to write for their series *Philosophical Outsiders*, as well as for their feedback on an early draft of the material, and to the reader for Oxford University Press, David Jackson, for an extremely helpful set of comments. An early version of Chapter 1 was delivered as the keynote lecture at a conference hosted by the Ramakrishna Mission Institute of Culture, Kolkata, in December 2022, and I thank the organizers, Nirmalya Chakraborty and Swami Tadvratananda, as well as the audience, for their very constructive feedback. I presented an earlier version of material as the Kennedy Lecture at Queen's University, Kingston in December 2023, and thank the members of the audience for keen advice. A version of Chapter 4 was presented at the international congress "Variations on Fernando Pessoa: From Presence to Contemporary Literature in Portuguese," which took place at the National Library of Portugal in June 2023. I must thank Jerónimo Pizarro for his kind invitation to participate, and Paulo de Medeiros and Bartholomew Ryan for their excellent comments. Chapter 7 was originally published in Bartholomew Ryan, Giovanbattista Tusa, and António Cardiello, eds., *Fernando Pessoa and Philosophy: Countless Lives Inhabit Us* (Rowman & Littlefield, 2021). Chapter 8 is based on an essay originally published as "Cosmic Consciousness" in *The Monist* 105 (2022). I am grateful to the publishers for permission to reuse these materials here. I am also very grateful to Austin Simões Gomes for helping me with translations of those of Pessoa's texts that are neither written in, nor previously translated into, English. In January 2024 I organised a seminar at Goa University, India, entitled

Fernando Pessoa: A Poet's Creed. I would like to thank everyone who participated, especially Koshy Tharakan, Dhruv Usgaonkar, David Jackson, Bartholomew Ryan, Anil Kumar Yadav, Loraine Alberto, and G. Tarun.

Introduction

Imagine, if you will, coming back as a fly. What are you really imagining? Perhaps what you see is being in a fly's body, with a fly's ability to, well, fly, and a fly's greater range of points of view on its (your) surroundings. You take up less space, and there is this irritatingly uncertain buzzing noise following you around, but essentially it's you incarnated in the body of a fly. Or perhaps what you imagine is actually becoming a fly, with a fly's appetites for gone-off food, a fly's more limited cognitive skill set, and its restricted emotional and intellectual life, but extraordinary powers of locomotion and unusual forms of sense perception. When you imagine in this way, your entire outlook, your way of being in the world, your emotional, cognitive, and sensory landscape, is different. Let me say, in short, your *bearing*. In either case you are, as philosophers say, imagining what it is like "from the inside" to be a fly. Your imagined experience is from the perspective of a fly, rather than one in which you look upon your fly-self from, as it were, an external vantage point (see Vendler 1979, 161; Kind and Kung 2016, 4). It is immersive. Yet imagining from the inside is, by itself, comparatively undemanding. You imagine flying "from the inside," for example, if you imagine the air flowing past and the ceiling coming towards you, and you can imagine doing that while in your own body. Imagining yourself immersively and differently embodied is already a more involved feat of imagination; imagining yourself immersively, differently embodied, *and* having a different bearing is more challenging still.

The distinction between immersively imagining being differently embodied and immersively imagining having a new

Fernando Pessoa. Jonardon Ganeri, Oxford University Press. © Oxford University Press 2024.
DOI: 10.1093/oso/9780197636688.003.0001

bearing crops up often in Indian stories about reincarnation. An *avatāra*—the word "avatar" is now a familiar one in the English language—is a god descended down to earth. But are we talking about our same old god in a new, human body, or is it that the god has become human, which, for a god, is presumably quite a lot like a human being becoming a fly? In the millennium-old *Mokṣopāya*, a great Kashmiri philosophical storybook better known as the *Yogavāsiṣṭha*, a doe falls asleep and "sees herself as" a bee. Is the story inviting us to imagine the doe as herself in apian form, or are we meant to suppose that the doe now sees herself as a bee inside and out? In another Indian story from a different source, the sage Nārada is made by Viṣṇu to see himself as a woman called Saubhāgyasundarī, forgetting all about his former male life, and the same question arises. Is it Nārada himself in a woman's body, or does Nārada now think himself to be Saubhāgyasundarī? It is relevant here that the same word, *avatāra*, is also used to refer to an actor's entrance from the wings, stepping not just *onto* the stage but also *into* a part. I believe that, more often than not, such stories are not just about body-swapping but also about having a new cognitive and affective bearing. Something more than mere incarnation or reincarnation is going on.

The early twentieth-century Portuguese poet Fernando Pessoa's curiosity about the reach of the imagination and the shifting sands of identity began early in life and remained the one constant preoccupation in this most creatively fluid of writers (for a comprehensive account of his life, consult Richard Zenith's magisterial biography [Zenith 2021], and for a survey of his work, see Bartholomew Ryan's brilliant new overview [Ryan 2024]). Pessoa had no trouble in imagining himself to be a fly:

> Who knows for what supreme forces—gods or demons of Truth in whose shadow we roam—I may be nothing but a shiny fly that alights in front of them for a moment or two? A facile hypothesis? Maybe. But I didn't think: I felt. It was carnally, directly,

> with profound and dark horror that I made this ludicrous comparison. I was a fly when I compared myself to one. I really felt like a fly when I imagined I felt like one. And I felt I had a flyish soul, slept flyishly and was flyishly withdrawn. And what's more horrifying is that I felt, at the same time, like myself. I automatically raised my eyes towards the ceiling, lest a lofty wooden ruler should swoop down to swat me, as I might swat that fly. (Pessoa 2002, #334)

Mostly, though, Pessoa wanted to imagine himself to be a different person—to have another self—while continuing, necessarily, to be himself. Over time he imagined himself to be more than a hundred different people, even if only three of his other selves were fully rounded out: Alberto Caeiro, Álvaro de Campos, and Ricardo Reis, three great poets of the Portuguese language. For above all Pessoa wanted to multiply himself, to "be plural like the universe!," as he once jotted down in a memo to self on a scrap of paper (Pessoa 1966, 94). Imagining being a virtual other is a way to achieve plurality, a feat he repeated a hundred times over and thrice in extreme detail. The goal, as he has Campos say in "Time's Passage," one of his most celebrated poems, is to feel everything in every way:

> To feel everything in every way,
> To live everything from all sides,
> To be the same thing in all ways possible at the same time,
> To realize in oneself all humanity at all moments
> In one scattered, extravagant, complete, and aloof moment.
> (Pessoa 1998, 146)

Pessoa vows to "be plural like the universe!" and seeks to achieve this in not one but two ways. The first is through a mechanism of self-estrangement: the subject of experience becomes, inside the virtual reality of a poem, another. The name Pessoa gives this mechanism is *heteronymy*, which is not merely having another name but rather having the name of another. Heteronyms are imagined minds, simulated selves, subjective artefacts, made-up "individuated points of view" (Zenith 2021, xxix), and no less real for that. And as if imagining being someone else (invariably a fabricated other, not an actual other person, for I am the prop in these games of make-believe about myself) were not hard enough, Pessoa went even further and claimed that there is a higher level of what he describes as "dreaming for metaphysical minds." He believed that he could, in very rare moments, or at least as a conceptual possibility, imagine being not one but many different people at the same time: "The highest stage of dreaming is when, having created a picture with various figures whose lives we live all at the same time, *we are jointly and interactively all of those souls.* This leads to an incredible degree of depersonalization and the reduction of our spirit to ashes" (Pessoa 2002, 405). This second attempt to achieve plurality within himself is through a mechanism of duplication, and the idea is a running theme in Pessoa's work right from the very beginning. It is already there in his first published story, from 1913, "The Forest of Estrangement." The protagonist bifurcates into a man and a woman, with "the forest, the two walkers, and I, I, unsure of which one I was, or if I was both, or neither" (2002, #386). These two techniques of self-pluralization, which we might call *pluralization by self-estrangement* and *pluralization by living a life in parallel*, are the main topics of this book. According to Pessoa, to be plural is the aim of every great poet.

In his most philosophical moments, Pessoa does wonder what makes a person real: if having an individualized point of view is enough, then surely the virtual selves he imagines himself to become are as real as the actual self he is. Or should one say, rather, that this so-called actual self is just one more virtual self among the rest? The philosopher David Chalmers has argued that the virtual objects we see when we put on a VR headset and immerse ourselves in a virtual world are real. Granted, they are digital objects made out of information and generated by computers, but they are for all that as real as objects made out of protons and electrons. Chalmers calls this "Reality+" (Chalmers 2022). Pessoa is interested in a version of that question, which he examines most fully in one of his most philosophical writings, "Notes for the Memory of My Master Caeiro" (Pessoa 2001, 36–50). But he takes matters a step further, entertaining the intriguing idea that there are virtual subjects as well as virtual objects, so that in immersing oneself in a virtual reality generated by one's imagination one might also virtualize oneself. We might call Pessoa's philosophy *Reality++*. The avatars of computer simulations are just bodies, manipulated, controlled, and even inhabited, but by users who are the same within the simulation as without. Pessoa's imagined others are *avatāras* in the truest sense, not just bodies but bearings, ways of being in a world: "The author of these books cannot affirm that all these different and well-defined personalities who have incorporeally passed through his soul don't exist, for he does not know what it means to exist, nor whether Hamlet or Shakespeare is more real, or truly real," he writes (Pessoa 2001, 2). Reality++, in all its inherent plurality, is Pessoa's metaphysics of the virtual, his philosophy of self-estrangement, his purpose as a poet, and his reason to be alive.

Is Fernando Pessoa a philosophical poet? Or is he a poetic philosopher? He doesn't seem to have been too sure himself. "I am a poet animated by philosophy, not a philosopher with poetic faculties," he writes, suggesting that for him philosophy serves the interests of poetry, not the other way round. And yet this most elusive of writers will also declare that "poetry is predominant in [my] *Fictions of the Interlude*. In prose, it is more difficult to other oneself" (Pessoa 2001, 313). That makes it seem as if his poetry is, after all, serving a philosophical end. Not, to be sure, the philosophy of the academics, but rather philosophy in the sense in which Henri-Frédéric Amiel reports in his *Journal* of having entered into "philosophical experiences" by way of "mental transformations," experiments in depersonalization whose ambition is knowledge about the self (Amiel [1885] 1889). In that sense of philosophy, as the art of performing metaphysical experiments upon oneself, to other oneself philosophically is the purpose of poetry for Pessoa. Pessoa's endless voyages to inner landscapes precluded an active life. Indeed, what Richard Wollheim said of Amiel applies in good measure to Pessoa: "As he spends more and more of his energies in the investigation of his own thoughts and moods and feelings, he becomes so fascinated by the detail that self-examination brings to light that he has, first, little time, and, then, no taste, for the more strenuous pursuit of life. It is in such a posture that novels and journals of the first half of the nineteenth century depicted young men of an exaggerated sensibility and an analytic cast of mind: Adolphe, Armance, Dominique, Amiel" (Wollheim 1984, 162–163). Richard Zenith says that the journal of Amiel was a partial inspiration for *The Book of Disquiet* (Zenith 2021, 721) and describes Pessoa's poetic heteronyms as "the most spectacular manifestation of his experimental research in personal identity" (Zenith 2021, 143). Zenith returns to the same theme at the very end of his epic biography, his final assessment being that "Fernando Pessoa was an experimentalist, whose own life was the permanent subject of his research. Each of the heteronyms was an experiment, as was each of the philosophical, political, literary, and religious points of view that he successively adopted and successively abandoned. . . . All were experiments, most of whose procedures and results he recorded, like a scientist of love, of commerce, of religion, and so on" (2021, 931). Pessoa was, in Zenith's apt phrase, a "poet-scientist" (2021, 932).

Pessoa is a philosophical outsider in more ways than this one. He is outside any institution of philosophy, any university, and he is a member of no philosophical community. Though he is widely read in philosophy, his attempts to write formal philosophical essays are few and far between. He creates a philosophy by means of writing literature, and it is within his literature that his philosophy finds expression. The philosophy he does so develop makes him an outsider in still another sense, for it is a philosophy without clear debts in the history of philosophy, and a philosophy that left no footprint after his death. Outside the academy, outside history, and even outside himself—Pessoa is as much of a philosophical outsider as it is possible to be.

Pessoa's poetry is thus a poetry of immersion. Poems, for Pessoa, simulate virtual realities, realities in which I, the subject, am an immersed participant. Pessoa, restless voyager in these alternative landscapes of sensation, "precociously adept at envisioning realities" (Zenith 2021, 17), discovers there a way to make himself someone other than he is. In the virtual reality generated by a poem it is I who is immersed, at the centre, the one with reference to whom things are presented and events take place. It is I, and yet it is another I, a me who is not the me of the ordinary world outside the poem. I, but yet another I. Simply put, this is because a poem's purpose is not merely, or even, to describe what's there but to prescribe a way of being, a new modality of having a world in view. It's I because within the virtual reality generated by the poem the first-person perspective is mine; it's another I because the mode of being in the world, for this I in this poem, is entirely new. That's why it's easier to other oneself in poetry, because the transformation is not in *what* one sees but in *how* one sees it. In poems, we are not our ordinary selves; we are virtual subjects immersed in the world freshly seen. We may call these two dimensions of virtual subjectivity "immersive centrality" and "immersive for-me-ness," respectively. Immersive centrality is the idea that one inhabits a field perspective within the simulation; we shall later also refer to this as the positional conception of self. Immersive for-me-ness is the idea that how one experiences matters as much as what one experiences, and indeed is essential to being who one is. Later, we will explain this idea in terms of the notion of a mode of poetic attention. Attention in general structures experience into topic and background, and, as Lucy Alford has recently argued (Alford 2020), poetry does just this in particular ways. We shall also have to ponder a tricky question: what happens when attention turns inward, when the topic of my attention is myself?

So this book is about plural poets and poetic pluralities. It is about Fernando Pessoa and his orthonym "Fernando Pessoa himself." It is about Pessoa's literary concoctions, the master poet Alberto Caeiro and his disciples Álvaro de Campos and Ricardo Reis. It's also about a lineage in the history of ideas that runs from the *Bhagavad-gītā* through Whitman to Pessoa, and back again to India. And it's about the bardly collective that goes by the name "Vasiṣṭha," nominal author of the *Mokṣopāya*. For indeed in poetry it is easier "to other oneself" (Pessoa 2001, 313).

PART I
POETS AND PLURALS

1

Be Plural! A Poet's Creed

Keats: The Poet as Chameleon

In undertaking to "be plural like the universe!" (Pessoa 1966, 94), Fernando Pessoa was not the first to associate the creed of the poet with a demand to be many. We can better appreciate what makes Pessoa unique by way of a brief review of his premodern precursors. Already in a letter dated October 27, 1818, the Romantic poet John Keats had famously described the poet as a chameleon:

> As to the poetical Character itself (I mean that sort of which, if I am any thing, I am a Member . . .) it is not itself—it has no self—it is every thing and nothing . . . What shocks the virtuous philosopher, delights the camelion Poet. . . . A Poet is the most unpoetical of any thing in existence; because he has no Identity—he is continually in for—and filling some other Body—The Sun, the Moon, the Sea and Men and Women who are creatures of impulse are poetical and have about them an unchangeable attribute—the poet has none. (Keats 2002, 195)

A poet has no identity to call their own, meaning specifically no "unchangeable attribute." The poet is ever infilling a body and, like a chameleon, ever changing to fit in. What Keats' "chameleon conception" of the poet's oath to be plural amounts to is a certain claim about the relationship between mind and world: that, for a poet, the direction of fit must be from world to mind, that the mind of a poet fills whichever place it finds itself in. The chameleon conception has it that a poet has as many minds as there are embodied contexts,

Fernando Pessoa. Jonardon Ganeri, Oxford University Press. © Oxford University Press 2024.
DOI: 10.1093/oso/9780197636688.003.0002

because to think as a poet is to endlessly adapt oneself to circumstance. The world, Keats will say in a subsequent letter of April 21, 1819, is a "vale of soul-making." It is the world that gives identity to mind:

> Call the world if you Please "the vale of Soul-making." Then you will find out the use of the world. . . . I say "*Soul making.*" Soul as distinguished from an Intelligence—There may be intelligences or sparks of the divinity in millions—but they are not Souls till they acquire identities, till each one is personally itself. . . . How then are Souls to be made? How then are these sparks which are God to have identity given them—so as ever to possess a bliss peculiar to each one's individual existence? How, but by the medium of a world like this? (Keats 2002, 290)

A spark of conscious awareness is made into an individual self by the world it finds itself in; and if it is the poet's fate to roam throughout the entirety of the world in imagination, then, inevitably, the poet must have as many distinct "identities" as there are worldly contexts to infill. I-making is embodied immersion in an experienced world.

Though affirming that the poet has no "identity," in the specific sense of not having an "unchangeable attribute," Keats is not saying that the mind of a poet is empty. Some commentators have, though, been drawn to an analogy between Keats and Zen (e.g., Pachori 1996; Benton 1966; Davis 2019). So Bret Davis writes that "the chameleon poet prefers to let his empty mind fluidly reflect the kaleidoscope complexity of the phenomenal world" (Davis 2019, 6–7). Davis refers to T. S. Eliot in support of his reading, Eliot writing that the poet must effect a "continual surrender of himself . . . a continual self-sacrifice, a continual extinction of personality," such that his mind becomes like a "catalyst," a "medium in which special, or very varied, feelings are at liberty to enter into new combinations" (Eliot 2001, 104). Keats, though, is not saying that the poet's mind is empty; he is saying, instead, that it is not fixed. Just as at any given moment the chameleon takes on a colour so as to fit its surrounds, so too the poet takes on, in each varying situation, a "soul" that fits it. The comparison of Keats and Zen would work only if it makes sense to ask after the colour of the chameleon when it has no surroundings. But that is just to expose the way the supposed comparison misses the mark, for there is no sense in such a question, and the inference to the idea of "a chameleon without any colour" is a fallacy.

Shakespeare: The Protean Poet

A different direction of fit informs a second premodern take on the poet's oath to be plural. It begins life in William Hazlitt's lecture "Shakespeare's Genius," delivered in 1818, at just the same time Keats was penning his letters. "The striking peculiarity of Shakespeare's mind," Hazlitt writes,

> was its generic quality, its power of communication with all other minds—so that it contained a universe of thought and feeling within itself, and had no one peculiar bias, or exclusive excellence more than another. He was just like any other man, but that he was like all other men. He was the least of an egotist that it was possible to be. He was nothing in himself; but he was all that others were, or that they could become. He not only had in himself the germs of every faculty and feeling, but he could follow them by anticipation, intuitively, into all their conceivable ramifications, through every change of fortune or conflict of passion, or turn of thought. (Hazlitt 1818, 91–92)

Shakespeare, Hazlitt says,

> had only to think of any thing in order to become that thing, with all the circumstances belonging to it. When he conceived

> of a character, whether real or imaginary, he not only entered into all its thoughts and feelings, but seemed instantly, and as if by touching a secret spring, to be surrounded with all the same objects, "subject to the same skyey influences," the same local, outward, and unforeseen accidents which would occur in reality. (Hazlitt 1818, 93)

Hazlitt's Shakespeare has only to exercise his formidable powers of imagination, anticipation, and intuition in order to "become that thing," and in so doing to think what it thinks, feel what it feels, and in general experience the world as it does, from its perspective and with—in my terminology—its *bearing*. The guiding metaphor is that of the theatre, of an actor's ability to become the character whose part they play. The direction of fit is now not from world to mind but from actor to role. Shakespeare, as playwright and as actor, *becomes* the very character. Here again we find the poet described as everything and nothing, and here too the "nothing" is immediately qualified: it is a "nothing *in himself*," a lack of any fixed identity, not an empty nothingness. Shakespeare is nobody *in himself* and everybody *in potentia*. This is not the extinction of personality but its multiplication, and it is an immersive bearing, a way of being in the world, not merely a way of occupying a place.

The conception of the poet's oath embodied in the cult of Shakespeare as the universal poet finds an exceptional formulation in a short story by Jorge Luis Borges, titled, perhaps unsurprisingly, "Everything and Nothing." Borges writes, "Instinctively, he had already trained himself to the habit of feigning that he was somebody, so that his 'nobodiness' might not be discovered. In London, he found the calling he had been predestined to; he became an actor, that person who stands upon a stage and plays at being another person. . . . No one was as many men as that man—that man whose repertoire, like that of the Egyptian Proteus, was all the appearances of being" (Borges 1999, 319–320). Despite Borges' description of the actor's performance as a feign, the point is that Shakespeare-as-actor does become each of the characters he plays (see also Carlson 2008, 33–35). There are, of course, times when an actor is not onstage, and these moments are, as it were, blanks or gaps in the actor's personal history. Borges describes them as "a return to being a nobody," echoing George Bernard Shaw's conception of Shakespeare as someone "devoid of a soul" (Shaw 1931, 11); but perhaps it is better to say that the life of an actor or poet contains discontinuities and is not a seamless, continuous stream. During these interruptions, yes, the poet is not a somebody, but we should not fall into the error of reifying the in-between states under the label "poet-as-nobody." That's a version of the same mistake that leads to the comparison between Keats and Zen. It would be preferable to say that there are times when there is no poet. The point here is well made by Joshua Landy in an essay about *Hamlet*. "Hamlet," he writes,

> has many, many selves to which to be true. Pace Polonius, he has a major problem on his hands. The predicament is clearly a very bad one, but there is an ingenious solution on offer . . . [which is,] in a nutshell, *to live like an actor*. . . . [I]t means taking your many parts and giving each its day in the sun. It means identifying completely with one aspect of yourself at any given time. . . . Here are some things this kind of life is *not*. It is not, first of all, a matter of inventing a persona for the benefit of other people; we're talking here about a part that "passes show" [Landy inserts a footnote here that says it's not "about effects on an audience [but] about effects on one's own psyche"]. It is not, second, a matter of picking a single aspect and calling it "the real you." It is not, third, a matter of combining all the parts into a unified super-self. And it is certainly not a matter, lastly, of inventing yourself out of nothing: *each of those roles is a genuine part of you*, even if none of them exhausts who you are. This may be acting, but it's not *performance*. Instead, it is a matter of taking the many things you already are and giving each of them a proper run-out when its moment comes around. (Landy 2018, 178)

Pessoa: The Poet of Immersion

Against the background of these two premodern understandings of the poet's creed, Pessoa comes out with a radically new and modern one. "Be plural like the universe!" is his motto, and he enacts it by becoming a plurality of poets—the famous triplet in Portuguese literature, and a vast plurality of other individuated points of view too. What is now the direction of fit? In an important text written in English, Pessoa says that he loves "to admire the beauty of things, to trace in the imperceptible through the minute the poetic soul of the universe" (2001, 9). He continues with a fascinating and philosophically illuminating explanation of what poetry is: "For poetry is astonishment, admiration, as of a being fallen from the skies taking full consciousness of his fall, astonished about things. As of one who knew things in their souls, striving to remember this knowledge, remembering that it was not thus he knew them, not under these forms and these conditions, but remembering nothing more" (Pessoa 2001, 9–10). Poetry is astonishment, an astonishment of the sort one feels on encountering something for the first time, a childlike wonder at what there is, and finding in everything thus encountered a "deeper meaning" that seems to stem from an indeterminate sense of familiarity. And poetry is admiration, a respect for the beauty of all that the world contains. Astonishment and admiration are, first of all, both world-involving states of mind: we are astonished *by* or *at* something, and we feel admiration *for* something. Both are, moreover, affective states, emotions: one *feels* astonished and *feels* admiration. They are reactions to the world and not projections onto it, which is to say they are not primarily acts of creative imagination. And yet they are not passive reactions, as changing one's colour to fit one's environment might be considered to be. For although Pessoa's poet falls upon the world as if encountering it for the first time, he does so "taking full consciousness of his fall." That is to say, poetic admiration and poetic astonishment are fully self-conscious emotions, emotional states of the sort that one can be in only if one is aware of oneself being in them.

Poetry is a singling out of something in one's environment, the attention to it and the simultaneous attention to oneself in the act of attending to it. For, Pessoa adds, "my inner sense predominates in such a way over my five senses that I see things in this life—I do believe it—in a way different from other men. There is for me—there was—a wealth of meaning in a thing so ridiculous as a door-key; a nail on a wall; a cat's whiskers" (2001, 9). "There is," writes Pessoa,

> poetry in everything—in land and in sea, in lake and in riverside. It is in the city too—deny it not—it is evident to me here as I sit: there is poetry in this table, in this paper, in this inkstand; there is poetry in the rattling of the cars on the streets, in each minute, common, ridiculous motion of a workman, who the other side of the street is painting the sign-board of a butcher's shop. (2001, 10)

Anything, however mundane or seemingly insignificant, can serve as the theme of poetic astonishment and admiration. Poetic astonishment and poetic admiration are names for those states of mind whereby one not only sees things in the world as if for the first time but also "sees in" those things other meanings, meanings that perhaps go unseen by those who are less self-aware.

All this is already a far cry from the negative capabilities of Keats and the prodigious feats of imagination Hazlitt attributes to Shakespeare. The direction of fit, I suggest, is now from attention to subjectivity. Pessoa does not say simply, "Be plural!" He says, "Be plural like the universe!" The universe is itself plural, and it is the plurality of the universe to which in some way the poet's oath to be plural is answerable. Yet the "vale of soul-making" is not now the world as such, the world in itself, but rather the world as an object of self-conscious attention. A paragraph in *The Book of Disquiet* describes the nature of the movement from attention to subjectivity even more vividly. The narrator, who is, of course, not quite Pessoa himself, says:

> The only way you can have new sensations is by forging a new soul. It's useless to try to feel new things without feeling them *in a new way*, and you can't feel in a new way without changing your soul. For things are what we feel they are—how long have you known this without yet knowing it?—and the only way for there to be new things, for us to feel new things, is for there to be some novelty in *how* we feel them. (2002, #301; italics added)

That is to say, a self is a way of feeling, a style of experiencing the world. If we combine this insight with the idea that poetry consists in astonishment and admiration, and remember that Pessoa pluralizes himself by becoming a plurality of poets, we arrive at the conclusion that there is a plurality of modes of astonishment and admiration, a plurality of ways of self-consciously attending to things, and that each such way of taking the world in view is also a way of having a different self or soul.

The poet becomes plural in sustaining a plurality of ways of attending to the world, each one a mode of actively seeing meaning in even the most mundane of things. The plurality of the subject is now, therefore, essentially a plurality of aesthetic encounters, because "attending to how one attends" is the mode of seeing appropriate to aesthetic experience: one sees a horse and is aware of how one sees it. As Bence Nanay has recently put it, "When we are looking at an apple, we can attend to the features of the apple. Or we can attend to the features of our experience of the apple. Or we can attend to both, and the relation between the two. Attending this third way is what I take to be a crucial (and maybe even close to universal) feature of aesthetic experience" (Nanay 2019, 38). Indeed, Nanay refers to Pessoa as an "authority" for this analysis of aesthetic experience.

There is another sort of twofoldness in attention, and it has to do with seeing representations. As Richard Wollheim writes, "That the seeing appropriate to representations permits simultaneous attention to what is represented and to the representation, to the object and to the medium, and therefore instantiates seeing-in rather than seeing-as, follows from a stronger thesis which is true of representations. The stronger thesis is that, if I look at a representation as a representation, then it is not just permitted to, but required of, me that I attend simultaneously to object and medium" (Wollheim 1980, 142). Wollheim invites us to consider "the difficulties that would have lain in store for us in our appreciation of poetry if it had been beyond our powers to have simultaneous awareness of the sound and the meaning of words. In painting and poetry twofoldness must be a normative constraint upon anyone who tries to appreciate works of those arts" (1980, 144). When Pessoa writes that "there is poetry in the rattling of the cars on the streets" he is, in Wollheim's terms, regarding the rattling of the cars as a representation. Wollheim calls this "seeing-in," and each of Pessoa's heteronyms is the personification of such a mode of seeing-in: Alberto Caeiro, the absolute objectivist who refuses to see anything in objects other than just what they are or to treat objects as representations of anything; Ricardo Reis, the Neoclassicist who sees in objects a lost Neoclassical order; and Álvaro de Campos, the lover of life who sees everything in every way and delights in everything. What those of us who aren't poets see in things are affordances and opportunities, to satisfy our desires and quell our fears. Each of these poets attends not just to what is seen in what but also to how such seeings-in are felt, and to the relation between the two. Each, that is to say, has a different mode of poetic attention and is, thereby, a different poet. To attend as Caeiro does, for example—that is to say, to attend *Caeiroesquely*—is to attend to the stone and to how one sees it without seeing anything in it at all. A mode of poetic attention is a way of attending to the relationship between what is seen-in what and how it is seen-in, and poets are individuated by the modes of poetic attention they employ. In so fulfilling the poet's oath to be plural, Pessoa says that he has made himself into "not just a writer but an entire literature" and that "the human author of these books has no personality of his own" (2001, 2–3). The point, again, is that "of his own" is a vital qualifier here: the claim is not that he has no personality at all but that he is, at any given moment of creative writing, the self whose mode of lived experience is encapsulated in that writing style.

It has been said that the years 1875 to 1927 were peak years for the modernist crisis in the hypothesis of an undivided and unitary self (Langbaum 1977, 216), a period into which Pessoa's own life nearly squarely falls. Yet Pessoa's philosophy of the plurality of the subject is quite different from that of other modernists of his period. In thinkers from Diderot to Proust and Nietzsche to Yeats, what we find is conception of mind as a hive of competing instincts and drives. "Man is a plurality of forces," says Nietzsche (Nietzsche 1980, 11:461). This is not a plurality of subjects but a single subject, one, however, that is now composite and fragmented. Diderot, Bernard Williams writes, "was always attracted to a picture of the self as something constantly shifting and reacting and altering; as a swarm of bees; as a clavichord or harp or other instrument, with the wind or some such force playing on it. It is near to the picture that Nietzsche offers, of our desires and needs groping around and reaching out inside us, as though they formed a kind of polyp" (Williams, 2002, 190). Nietzsche comes closer to Pessoa in his posthumously published fragments from 1885, writing that "the hypothesis of a single subject is perhaps not necessary; perhaps it is also permissible to assume a plurality of subjects, whose reciprocal play and struggle underlie our thinking and even our conscience?" (Nietzsche 1980, 11:650). In a similar vein, Marcel Proust reflects on "those innumerable and humble 'selves' that compose our personality" and refers to "a truly objective truth . . . namely that none of us is single, that each of us contains many persons who do not all have the same moral value" (Proust 1982, 3:605).

Pessoa's key departure from such sentiments consists in his insistence that there must always be what we might call a "frame of heteronymy," a context of simulation, expressed in such formulae as "In my dream . . . ," "In my poem . . . ," or "In my imagination . . ." When Pessoa writes poetry as the heteronym Alberto Caeiro, it is not the case that, sitting in his study, he has literally transformed himself into this other poet. No: it is that, in his dreaming, and in his writing, he has become Alberto Caeiro, imagining himself seeing the world in the manner Caeiro sees it. The idea that there is a frame of heteronymy is crucial in understanding Pessoa's project, and it is why Pessoan plurality has nothing to do with multiple personality disorder or the fragmentation of the self (see Ganeri 2021, 27–31). Needless to say, imagining *being* someone else is also a quite different sort of intellectual enterprise from imagining someone else, and Pessoa's heteronyms have little in common with the fin-de-siècle "imaginary portraits" of Walter Pater, such as "The Child in the House" (Pater 1878).

In "Notes for the Memory of My Master Caeiro," Campos is given to ask if there is anything more genuinely Fernando Pessoa than the "poetic intersections in which the narrator's state of mind is simultaneously in two states, in which the subjective and objective join together while remaining separate, and in which the real and the unreal merge in order to remain distinct? In these poems Fernando Pessoa made a veritable portrait of his soul. In that one, unique moment he succeeded in having his own individuality, such as he had never had before and can never have again, because he has no individuality" (Pessoa 2001, 50). The poet performs a sophisticated feat of dual attention, dividing his or her awareness between something in the world and his or her own subjective state in the act of attending. The poet attends to both the *what* of experience and the *how* of experience; how a thing shows up is just as important as which thing comes into view, for it is in this that its "deeper meanings" are to be found. "My attention floats between two worlds," Pessoa declares in the early story "In the Forest of

Estrangement" (Pessoa 2002, 417). In her important recent study of the forms of poetic attention, Lucy Alford likewise speaks of poetry's "double transitivity," where "the element of the imagination in poetry's transitive attention acknowledges the subject's active part in penetrating beyond direct perception, pushing into and opening the mystery objects hold in their modes of perceptual evasion" (Alford 2020, 27), and she proposes to parse the phrase "attending poetically" to mean "bringing formal attention to the ways in which attention is manipulated by the form of the language itself," where "the doubleness of 'attention to the form of attention' is intentional here and uniquely poetic in nature" (2020, 15). Indeed, Alford finds in Whitman the very idea I have identified in Pessoa, that the poet's creed to be plural is discharged through a multiplicity in the modes of self-conscious attention, Alford writing that "despite the plurality of Whitman's attention, there is a sense not of fragmentation but rather of manyness . . . [so that] the subject is constituted in the particularity of a given mode of attention. In Wallace Stevens' terms, 'I am what is around me' " (2020, 37). Alford's categorization of the forms of poetic attention under four broad headings—contemplation, desire, recollection, and imagination—constitutes a keen analysis of what are, for Pessoa, the vales of soul-making.

Missing from Alford's description, however, is any reference to astonishment or admiration, and these states would fall under a fifth heading: emotion. That certain emotions are themselves forms of poetic attention, and indeed that they are the highest of all such forms, is one of Pessoa's key innovations and insights. Astonishment means something like "surprise in recognition": I expect something I see to be a certain way, but it presents itself as otherwise. Expectation is linked to background knowledge and so to memory, as indeed Pessoa intimates. The surprise is due to an incongruity between my expectation and what I perceive as the case. I come across something in the world and it astonishes me: I had expected it, possibly at some subliminal level, to be quite otherwise.

So the emotion of astonishment requires an expectation, a perception, and an awareness of their incongruence. Admiration is more a term of appraisal, itself a key component in emotion according to most theories of the emotions. To feel admiration for something is to evaluate it as excelling in some way. One admires the beauty in a sunset; one admires the courage in a deed.

What we are led to say, following Pessoa, is that attending poetically is seeing in a thing something one did not expect and yet appraises positively. To be conscious of one's surprise and admiration is to acknowledge this something new in the thing one sees, and so to discover in it a "deeper meaning." In enjoining the poet to "be plural," what the poet's creed demands is that the poet cultivate the ability to be surprised by the world in as many ways as possible, and to discover ever new ways to find something of beauty or value in this surprise. All in all, a far richer and more fascinating depiction of the cognitive life of the poet than simply as someone engaged in superhuman feats of prodigious imagination. Pessoa has Bernardo Soares speak of "the world's astonishing objectivity" (Pessoa 2002, 444), and he says himself that "everything, for [the pagan], has an astonishing immediate reality, and he feels fellowship with each thing when he sees it, and friendship when he touches it" (Pessoa 2001, 152). "The astonishing reality of things," writes the poet Caeiro, "is my discovery every day" (Pessoa 2006, 58). Astonishment is an emotion directed towards the immediate world, while fellowship and friendship are nothing if not avowals of admiration.

2
Self-Estrangement

In the Forest of Estrangement

Pessoa's first published piece of creative writing, from 1913 and already announced as a trailer for his never-finished *Book of Disquiet*, is entitled "In the Forest of Estrangement" (2002, 417–423). As he would later caution readers:

> Don't imagine that I write just to write, or to publish, or to produce art. I write because this is the final goal, the supreme refinement, the temperamentally illogical refinement, of my cultivation of states of mind and feeling. If I take one of my sensations and unravel it so as to use it to weave the inner reality I call "The Forest of Estrangement" . . . , you can be sure I don't do it for the sake of a lucid and shimmering prose . . . but to give complete exteriority to what is interior, thereby enabling me to realize the unrealizable, to conjoin the contradictory and, having exteriorized my dream, to give it its most powerful expression as pure dream. (Pessoa 2002, 444)

The forest is for Pessoa a metaphor for an artificial reality: "We inhabit dreams, we are shadows roaming through impossible forests, in which the trees are houses, customs, ideas, ideals and philosophies" (2002, #178). To roam about in such a forest is to live as another, as a virtual self experiencing "from the inside" a virtual world. For the forest is a dream, and the "I" who treads its paths is not Fernando Pessoa himself, half asleep in his cosy alcove, but another "I," one he has created by virtualizing himself. "And just as we

Fernando Pessoa. Jonardon Ganeri, Oxford University Press. © Oxford University Press 2024.
DOI: 10.1093/oso/9780197636688.003.0003

were thinking of mentioning the forest, it looms once more before us, as dense as ever but now more anguished with our anguish, and sadder with our sadness. Our idea of the real world vanishes in its presence like a dissipating fog, and once more I possess myself in my wandering dream, set in that mysterious forest" (2002, 420).

Pessoa suggests that the two realities, one actual and the other virtual, the realities of the alcove and the forest, can even intersect hypnagogically: "This new reality—that of a strange forest—makes its appearance without effacing the reality of my warm alcove. The two realities coexist in my captivated attention, like two mingled vapours." And again: "Sometimes in that forest, where from afar I see and feel myself, a light breeze spreads a mist, and that mist is the dark, clear vision of the alcove where I exist in reality, among these hazy pieces of furniture and drapes and nocturnal torpor. Then the breeze subsides and the landscape of that other world returns to being completely and exclusively itself" (2002, 417–418).

Notice that we have here a frame of heteronymy, indicated by the phrase "in that forest . . . ," and we have two distinct uses of the first-person pronoun, the first to refer to the immersed subject in the forest and the second to the simulator in his alcove, the one who "exists in reality." In still another fragment (and *The Book of Disquiet* is a book of fragments), Pessoa describes the protagonist's experience from what is clearly an immersed point of view: "And besides the leaves under our feet we could hear, in the wind's rough accompaniment, the constant falling of other leaves, or sounds of leaves, wherever we walked or had walked. . . . And always, as if surely there were a sun and day out there, one could see clearly—to nowhere—in the clamorous silence of the forest" (2002, #386). Within this forest of experience, everything is presented to a particular point of view, from the positioning of the leaves to the location of the sounds and the direction of the walk.

The protagonist is soon accompanied by a mysterious female double, about whom I will say more later. This doubling is Pessoa's first exploration of what I earlier dubbed "pluralization by living a life in plural." More importantly, as he, or they, walk in the forest, smell the flowers, and hear the cries of the birds, the "I" is not the same one as the "I" who, from the comfort of his alcove, writes the forest into being. This is what I have referred to as pluralization by self-estrangement ("self-estrangement" is a term Richard Zenith also uses, to describe Pessoa's comment in a letter dated November 19, 1914, that "I am no longer me" [Zenith 2021, 433]). Pessoa has not yet—but soon will—coin the neologism "heteronym." A heteronym is another I; not merely another name for myself, my heteronym is another me, who is nevertheless not me. What are we to make of this bizarre-sounding, seemingly paradoxical idea? How can there be another me who is not me? Hasn't Pessoa been taught that nothing can be identical to something other than itself, and so that for me to try to imagine that I am, for example, Napoleon is to attempt to imagine what is metaphysically impossible?

"Something Obscure in the Centre of My Being"

All is not lost. In his splendid book *Dream, Death, and the Self*, Jeremy Valberg asks us to consider the following case: "Suppose I have a dream in which there are two individuals (human beings), X and JV. Yet in the dream I am not JV but X (X is me). This seems possible, but what does it mean? Not that, in the dream, JV was X. In the dream, JV and X are distinct individuals. JV is in the dream, but in the dream JV is not me. In the dream I am a human being other than the human being that I am. . . . In the first-person case, given that JV and X are distinct individuals in the dream, there still exists the possibility that in the dream I am X" (Valberg 2007, 62). We are to suppose I have a dream in which I and a friend are present. What is peculiar about this dream, however, is that *in the dream* I am my friend, and what I dream is, for instance, that sitting at a table is a person, JV who is me. Notice how closely the sentence "In the dream I am a human being other than the human being that I am" echoes Pessoa's formulation of heteronymy, an I who I am not. There is a frame of heteronymy and an immersed subject. Why is it that the sentence does not simply affirm that in the dream Valberg is not Valberg? The puzzle is to know what makes it the case that in the dream I am X, not JV: on what grounds should we answer the question "Which one is me?" As Valberg puts it, "Consider the set of human beings in the cafe. One of them—this one—is the one I call 'me.' On what basis do I select him? What makes *him me*?" (2007, 65). And he makes the following very helpful suggestion: "We may understand the possibility as follows. In the dream it is X, not JV, who occupied the subject position—the position occupied by JV in reality. That is, it is X, not JV, who is at the centre of the dream. In reality, JV is the one at the centre: JV is me. In the dream, X occupies the position at the centre: in the dream X is me" (2007, 66–67). Valberg's proposal is to call attention to what he labels a *positional use* of the first person, distinct from its mundane use as an indexical, and a corresponding *positional conception* of self. Using "I" positionally, I am the one to whom all this is presented, the one to whom every phenomenal property is directed, or, as Valberg puts it, the one who is "at the centre" of the manifold of presentation, which he calls the experiential horizon, and which Pessoa calls the forest. "The positional conception of self," Valberg explains,

> is the conception of a position, namely, a position within THIS, the personal horizon (my horizon). . . . The main idea is that it is by virtue of occupying the subject position that a particular entity, a particular human being, is "me," the one that "I am." Thus the picture contains three elements: the entity that I am; the position by occupying which that entity is the one that I am; and the subject matter, my horizon, within which this position is defined. . . . This possibility, though it may be in various ways problematic, does not contradict the necessity of identity. It is an

experiential possibility, one that can be exhibited in imagination. (2007, 264)

The reason the envisaged possibility does not contradict the necessity of identity is that it turns out not to involve identity after all, surface grammar notwithstanding. What it claims is that a certain phenomenological property, the property "being the one at the centre of this field of experience," is instantiated in a given individual: "If I assert 'JV is me,' we may take 'is me' as replaceable by 'figures as the one at the centre of my horizon,' i.e. as a predicate. . . . To spell out the meaning of the predicate is to spell out the phenomenology of the subject position, i.e. the positional conception of the self" (2007, 334). Again, "Assuming the positional use of the first person, the meaning of 'JV is me (the one that I am)' is: JV figures as the one at the centre of my horizon. The 'is' in the expression 'is me,' then, is not the 'is' of identity, nor is 'me' a singular term; rather the whole expression 'is me' functions as a predicate" (2007, 336). So if in the forest the protagonist were to say, "I hear the leaves falling," the first-person pronoun would refer to whosoever it was at the centre of the immersed point of view, the point with reference to which all the happenings in the forest present themselves as taking place. When, on the other hand, Pessoa writes "of the alcove where I exist in reality," the first person is being employed in its everyday use, as an indexical that refers to whoever utters it. The mere fact that it is Fernando Pessoa who is imagining the forest does not necessitate that he is the one at the phenomenal centre in the forest. Another name for positionality is immersion, and what Valberg has, in effect, provided is an explanation of how the reference of "I" gets fixed in immersive centrality. In Mark Johnston's summary of the view, we have "distinguished two uses of first-person pronouns: a straightforward indexical use that refers simply to the human being that one is, a use characteristic of self-introductions and the like, and a truly subjective use where an interesting subjective property, the property of being at the centre of a given arena [of presence], is in play" (Johnston 2010, 192).

There is good evidence that Pessoa is fully conscious of the distinction between indexical and positional uses of the first person. He writes, "I'm always here inside, enclosed by high walls, on the private estate of my consciousness of me" (2002, #338), a clear articulation of the idea of immersion. Speaking of his phenomenological existence as his "being," he says, "There remains something obscure / In the centre of my being" (Pessoa 1973, 92). Elsewhere he appeals directly to the idea of a phenomenological centre, several times exploiting the metaphor of a well and its walls to describe the structure of the field of experience:

> My soul is a black whirlpool, a vast vertigo circling a void, the racing of an infinite ocean around a hole in nothing. And in these waters which are more a churning than actual waters float the images of all I've seen and heard in the world—houses, faces, books, boxes, snatches of music and syllables of voices all moving in a sinister and bottomless swirl. And amid all this confusion I, what's truly I, am the centre that exists only in the geometry of the abyss: I'm the nothing around which everything spins, existing only so that it can spin, being a centre only because every circle has one. I, what's truly I, am a well without walls but with the wall's viscosity, the centre of everything with nothing around it. (2002, #262)

Or, again: "This is my morality, or metaphysics, or me: passer-by of everything, even of my own soul, I belong to nothing, I desire nothing, I am nothing—just an abstract centre of impersonal sensations, a fallen sentient mirror reflecting the world's diversity" (2002, #208). As the centre of a well is that to which the surfaces of the well face, so the sensations that constitute the phenomenal field face towards a phenomenal centre, and the positional use of "I" is its use to refer to the one, whoever it is, who is at this centre: "I'm the one here in myself, it's me" (2006, 240).

Richard Zenith, in his magnificent biography, has many astute observations to make about Pessoa's philosophy of self. He says, first of all, that the just-quoted sentences in #262 "evince an uncannily Buddhist view of the world" (Zenith 2021, 789), an affinity I have explored in detail elsewhere (Ganeri 2021, chap. 15). More evidently evincing an affinity with Buddhism are the lines in poem 45 of Alberto Caeiro's *The Keeper of Sheep*:

> A row of trees in the distance, toward the slope . . .
> But what is a row of trees? There are just trees.
> "Row" and the plural "trees" are names, not things.
> (Pessoa 2006, 41; ellipsis in original)

These lines are bound to remind us of the Buddhist argument that persons are just like chariots, their names mere appellations where all that there is are axles, wheels, planks, and so on (see Horner 1963). Also quasi-Buddhist is Galen Strawson's "pearl view" of the self—that diachronic personal identity consists in a temporal string of momentary selves (Strawson 1999). It is fascinating to note that exactly such a view, and even the very metaphor used to describe it, is anticipated by Pessoa, who, as Álvaro de Campos, writes, "Or are we—all the I's that I was here or that were here— / A series of bead-beings joined together by a string of memory" ("Lisbon Revisited (1926)," in Zenith 2021, 672). "I have never settled down to . . . an opinion outlasting the transient minute in which it was held," he writes the same year in a letter to a newspaper (see Zenith 2021, 683). Zenith finds Pessoa, in a poem written on September 20, 1933, "*exulting* in his permanently shifting identity: 'To travel! . . . To be forever someone else. . . . To belong not even to me!,'" rightly commenting that in dispensing with the notion of an enduring self, "'Pessoa,' according to this poem, is whatever he happens to be at the moment" (Zenith 2021, 836). Or as

Zenith puts it elsewhere: "Pessoa's particular genius condemned him to being entirely whatever person he was, during the brief time he was that particular person. The 'real Fernando Pessoa' was always someone else" (2021, 669). In particular, when Pessoa uses the term "depersonalization," the meaning is not that there is an impersonal substrate of conscious experience, but rather that experiences are always felt as owned by a dramatized other. This is what his neologism "heteronym" intends to capture: "A heteronymous work involved more than just an invented name; it required the author to write 'outside his own person'" (Zenith 2021, 718). Pessoa "typically relied on his own thoughts and emotions for the raw material of his poetry, but he removed, distorted, or transformed their original contexts, in a process he described as 'depersonalization'" (Zenith 2021, 913), "having developed an extraordinary, Whitmanesque capacity for dramatically marrying himself to the scenes and characters described in his poems, while remaining completely detached" (Zenith 2021, 435). He is actor, character, playwright, spectator, and stage, all at once. The poem "Countless Lives," written on November 13, 1935, in Pessoa's last year, a year in which he tries to provide a definitive articulation of his literary project, is most clearly "Fernando Pessoa telling us what it means for him to be a poet of many voices and what it means to *be*, period" (Zenith 2021, 921). Experiences felt as owned by another are, in one sense, "feigned" experiences, as Pessoa put it in his "Autopsychography," which "is not about feigning what one *doesn't* feel so as to create convincing characters, be they Hamlets or heteronyms; it is about feigning [inventing, simulating] what one *does* feel, so as to convert it into literature" (Zenith 2021, 778).

What imagining oneself as another amounts to, therefore, is imagining a virtual reality centred on a position, and it will then follow from the semantics of the positional use of "I" that I am the one at the centre, someone who is quite possibly different from the one who is performing the act of imagination. That other one is picked out by an indexical use of "I" instead. As Mark Johnston puts it, "It's is a contingent claim, and one that is not always true, that in my dreams I am the human being Johnston" (Johnston 2010, 150). In such a situation, one is estranged from oneself. For an exact Pessoan replica of Valberg's example, we need only consider again what he writes in the essay "Notes for the Memory of My Master Caeiro." The essay describes a meeting between Caeiro, Fernando Pessoa, and the other heteronyms, all as related by Álvaro de Campos in the first person. So Campos writes, "If I remember correctly we got on to this subject because of a tangential remark made by Fernando Pessoa" (Pessoa 2001, 42). The "I" here is used positionally, and it refers to Campos; Campos is the one at the centre of the presented arena of events. Fernando Pessoa is there, just as Valberg is there in his dream. But when Pessoa imagines this get-together of the heteronyms, he is imagining himself as Campos in conversation with Fernando Pessoa, who is also present. He is imagining being Campos talking with Pessoa. As the poet Gwendolyn MacEwen would put the idea concisely in her poem entitled, "The Carnival," "Who am I, and who / Lives in the carnival behind my eye?" (1999, 45). Indeed, the imagined arena of experience is often much more like a carnival than a forest or a field.

Imagining Being Another

I said that we need to distinguish between two ways of imagining being someone else: imagining being in another *body*, an imagined reincarnation, and imagining having a different *bearing*, bearing being a matter of an entire way of being in the world, cognitive and affective. We must try, now, to make this distinction sharper. In both cases we have, first of all, a virtual reality *environment*. This goes by different names: it is Valberg's "horizon," Johnston's "arena of presence"; for Pessoa it is a "forest" or, more frequently, a "landscape" (see Ganeri 2021, 78–86). There is, second, a *generator* of this virtual reality environment. For it is a simulation, and simulations by their very nature are artificially made. Most contemporary work on virtual reality is concerned with computer-generated simulations, but for Pessoa the virtual reality environment that is the forest, or the landscape, is generated by his imagination (he calls it *sonhando*, "dreaming"). Finally, in both cases we need an *immersed* subject, a subject who occupies a first-person point of view within the simulated virtual reality environment and who interacts with the virtual objects within it.

The distinction between being in a body and having a bearing is a distinction *within* the concept of immersion. Valberg's analysis of centrality makes immersion entirely a matter of embodiment. He writes, "The human being (body) that is 'me' ('mine') is the one that is perceptually present in a unique way (perceptual centrality); is the one that is the locus of feeling (centrality of feeling); and is the one whose movements figure as willed (volitional centrality)" (Valberg 2007, 271). As far as Pessoa is concerned, however, my body is not me, and an account of what makes this body mine cannot serve as a full analysis of what makes this person me. What does it take for Pessoa to imagine himself "from the inside" as Caeiro? Let us consider a recent discussion about a somewhat related case—namely, that of imagining oneself to be Napoleon. There is, in the literature on imagination, a discussion of the nature of *de se* imagining in general, and the idea of imagining being someone else in particular. Important contributions have been made by philosophers, including Bernard Williams, Zeno Vendler, Kendall Walton, and François Recanati.

In a famous essay, "Imagination and the Self," Bernard Williams writes:

> "I might have been somebody else" is a very primitive and very real thought; and it tends to carry with it an idea that one knows what it would be like for this I to look out on a different world, from a different body, and still be the same I. To start at the easiest place, we know perfectly well that a great deal of what we are,

> in terms of memory, character, and bodily development, is the product of accidental factors which we can readily conceive to have been otherwise. . . . If we press this hard enough, we readily get the idea that it is not necessary to being *me* that I should have any of the individuating properties that I do have, this body, these memories, etc. And for some of them, such as the body, we may think that it is not necessary to have one at all; and, quite readily, we might not have any memories. (Williams 1973, 40–41)

He continues:

> I have used several times the formula "imagining myself doing, being, etc., such and such," where this "myself" is, roughly, my ordinary self . . . But where the question is of imagining being, for instance, Napoleon, the formula "imagining *myself* being Napoleon" is possibly misleading. It draws us near to a formula that may also be used, and which may be even more misleading—though misleading, of course, only when I start reflecting on it: the formula "imagining that I am (or was) Napoleon. " For with regard to this formula, we may feel bound to ask what this "I" is that turns up inside the expression of what I imagine. If it is the ordinary empirical one, as I am, what I imagine seems to be straightforwardly self-contradictory, which stops me in my tracks; and this will not do, for I know that, in imagining being Napoleon, I am not stopped in my tracks. . . . . The mode of imagining appropriate to these fantasies, when they are not stopped in their tracks, is least misleadingly expressed as "imagining being Napoleon": what this represents, the fantasy enactment of the role of Napoleon, is the only mode that has the power to sustain the speculations we have been discussing at all. And this mode, properly understood, does not introduce a further "me" to generate these difficulties: there are only two persons involved in this, as I said, the real me and Napoleon. It is as

> unproblematic that I can imagine being Napoleon as that Charles Boyer could act the role of Napoleon. (Williams 1973, 44–45)

So for Williams, imagining *myself* as someone else can only mean imagining being someone else, and that is very much like playing a part onstage or the fantasy enactment of a role.

Zeno Vendler restates Williams' argument, perhaps with greater perspicuity, employing the metaphor of an "intersubjective transference" into an "alien perspective":

> By the signal feat of intersubjective transference I can imagine being you, Napoleon, or even Napoleon at the battle of Waterloo. . . . And the only way of doing this is by imagining being you, seeing the world from an alien perspective. . . . "But," you object, "how can you imagine being me, or worse, being Napoleon, since you are not, and this, we are told is a necessary truth. Therefore your alleged feat of transference would consist in imagining something impossible." Not so, I reply, for I do not try to imagine *myself* being you, Napoleon, or even simply *myself* being at the battle of Waterloo. . . . What I can do is imagine being Napoleon, i.e. having the experiences he must have had on the battlefield, or on other occasions. (Vendler 1979, 172–173; cf. Vendler 1984, 35–41)

In his classic book, *Mimesis and Make-Believe*, Kendall Walton develops the basic idea in a somewhat different direction. He writes:

> One can imagine being Napoleon, as we say, and seeing a rhinoceros through his eyes. . . . The best way to avoid supposing that one imagines a metaphysical impossibility, if one feels obliged to avoid it, is something like this: One imagines (oneself) seeing a rhinoceros. And by means of this first-person self-imagining one imagines Napoleon to be seeing a rhinoceros. (1990, 51–53)

Yet, imagining being Napoleon is not the same as imagining Napoleon, and Walton's attempt to preserve the *de se* element by adding an additional conjunct seems somewhat ad hoc. In an insightful discussion, François Recanati argues that we must draw a distinction between two sorts of *de se* imagining, in only one of which the imaginer's self is involved. A normal case of *de se* imagining is evaluated with respect to the imagining subject. If I say, "Pessoa imagines writing a poem," then Pessoa, despite not being an explicit element in the imagined content, is nevertheless the person with respect to whom the truth or falsity of what I say is accountable. In cases such as imagining being Napoleon penning a letter, on the other hand, the imagining subject does not enter the picture at all, and instead it is to Napoleon himself that the imagined property is ascribed. Recanati calls this "quasi-*de se*" imagining, and says that he will use the term "to refer to the type of thought one entertains when one imagines, say, being Napoleon. The type of imagining is clearly first-personal, yet the imaginer's self is not involved—not even at the 'evaluation' stage. The properties that are imaginatively represented are not ascribed to the subject who imagines them, but to the person whose point of view she espouses" (Recanati 2007, 207). Quasi-*de se* imagination is supposed to be analogous to quasi-memory, which is remembering doing something but without self-attribution. Recanati's idea is that in imagining being someone else there is an espoused point of view, which is not one's own point of view, and the ascription of imagined psychological properties is made with respect to it.

What about Pessoa? When Pessoa imagines Caeiro writing a poem, it is Caeiro's point of view that is espoused, and it is to Caeiro that the property of writing a poem is ascribed. So does heteronymic imagining (Pessoan "dreaming") also fall into the category of the quasi-*de se*? The reason this suggestion fails is that there is a subtle but vital difference between the case of Bernard Williams imagining being Napoleon Bonaparte penning a letter and the case of Fernando Pessoa imagining being Alberto Caeiro writing a poem. The difference is that Caeiro is not merely another person, whose point of view Pessoa has espoused, but a new version of Pessoa, created by Pessoa himself as an alter ego. It is impossible, therefore, to describe heteronymic imagining as a case where "the imaginer's self is not involved." It isn't simply that Pessoa imagines being Caeiro; rather, when he imagines Caeiro he imagines Caeiro to be an alter ego of himself.

Let us agree that ordinary *de se* imagining is imagining doing or experiencing, where there is an implicit anaphoric pronoun (sometimes called "PRO") serving as the subject of the infinitive. Why not regard imagining *being* as a sort of special case of imagining *doing* and *experiencing*? That is to say, imagining being Caeiro is imagining being in the world as Caeiro is, doing and experiencing things in the manner that exemplifies Caeiro's manner of being. When Pessoa imagines being Caeiro seeing a stone, what we should say is that he is imagining seeing a stone in a Caeiroesque manner, or Caeiroesquely. To see a stone Caeiroesquely is to see it simply as a stone and not as a stand-in for anything else:

> I say of the stone, "It's a stone."
> I say of the plant, "It's a plant."
> I say of myself, "It's me."
> And I say no more. What more is there to say? (Pessoa 2006, 23)

So heteronymic imagining is not quasi-*de se* but genuine *de se* imagining. The point is just, to repeat what we said earlier in connection with the positional conception of "I," that the word "being" in "being Caeiro" must be construed not as an "is" of identity but as an "is" of predication. If that is right, then we should distinguish between two types of imagining being Napoleon, the case involving quasi-*de se* (with an "is" of identity) and the case involving genuine *de se* (with an "is" of predication). In the second case what one imagines is doing and experiencing Napoleonically. One can report one's imaginative feat by saying, "In my *de se* imagining, I was

Napoleon," where this is, of course, quite different from saying, "I imagined that I was Napoleon."

The difference between imagining being Caeiro seeing a stone and imagining being in Caeiro's body seeing a stone—that is, between what I am calling immersive for-me-ness and immersive centrality—is a difference in imagined manners of seeing: in the second case, although imagining being in Caeiro's body is sufficient for this to count as immersion, it is still a matter of imagining seeing the world *as myself*. Such manners of seeing are, for Pessoa, modes of poetic attention. Indeed, as Master Caeiro himself says: "What you call poetry is everything. And it's not even poetry: it's seeing" (Pessoa 2001, 40). To each different "self" there is a different way to find the reality of the world astonishing and admirable. "Our garden," says the protagonist of "In the Forest of Estrangement," "had flowers endowed with every kind of beauty: roses with ruffled edges, yellowish-white lilies, poppies that would remain hidden if their deep red didn't betray them, violets towards the verdant borders of the flower beds, delicate forget-me-nots, camellias with no scent . . . And above the tall grasses, the startled eyes of solitary sunflowers stared at us intently" (Pessoa 2002, 418; ellipsis in original). In the forest of estrangement, in the strangeness of the forest, there is astonishment in its existence and admiration for its beauty.

PART II

VARIETIES OF HETERONYMOUS EXPERIENCE

3
Artefact Minds

Simulacron-3

Fernando Pessoa dreams being Alberto Caeiro. In his dreams, Pessoa is Caeiro. Acts of self-estrangement always require the sort of context provided by the expression "in his dreams." I have called it the *frame* of heteronymy. Pessoa is immersed in a dream field of sensation. He is the one at its centre, and for that reason he can refer to himself, in the dream, as "I." So acts of self-estrangement also require immersion, a *centre* position in the forest of estranged sensation. In his dreams, Fernando Pessoa imagines himself as the one at the centre, but he also imagines himself being Alberto Caeiro. Imagining oneself as someone else is, I have claimed, a matter of imagining seeing and feeling the world in a different way, rather than simply seeing and feeling different things. For every new self, one might imagine oneself to be, there is a *way of seeing and feeling* one can imagine seeing and feeling by way of. Experiencing the world in a certain way is what I mean by a way of being in the world, and "having a self" is, plausibly, a good enough description of what being in the world in a given way amounts to. This is what I dubbed, at the beginning of this book, a cognitive and affective bearing. It is only when all three are present—a frame, a centre, and a bearing—that one can truly say, "In this dream, I am so-and-so." The imagination is just one method of generating such a simulation, though, and something similar will be true for any other simulation, be it a computer-generated virtual reality, the virtual reality of a poem or novel, or one of those simulations that, as we will see in subsequent

Fernando Pessoa. Jonardon Ganeri, Oxford University Press. © Oxford University Press 2024.
DOI: 10.1093/oso/9780197636688.003.0004

chapters, the gods are wont to impose upon us for what they consider to be educational reasons.

If we look very carefully, we can detect traces of heteronymy in Daniel F. Galouye's 1964 cult science fiction classic *Simulacron-3*, a novel whose primary aim is to explore the consequences of discovering that one is nothing more than a simulation in a virtual environment created by an electronic machine (an early anticipation of the so-called simulation hypothesis). Doug Hall, the story's protagonist, is the lead technician in a project to build such a machine: "We can electronically simulate a social environment. We can populate it with subjective analogs—reactional identity units" into which can even be programmed emotional characteristics. The inventor's "basic discovery" is that these "reaction entities weren't merely ingenious circuits in a simulectronic complex, but instead were real, living, thinking personalities. In his opinion, I'm sure, they actually existed. In a solipsistic world, perhaps, but never suspecting that their past experiences were synthetic, that their universe wasn't a good, solid, firm, materialistic one" (Galouye 1999, 9). And if they do become aware of the fact that their material basis is electrons in silicon circuit boards rather than organic molecules, what then? For Ashton, a reaction unit who does so become self-aware, the threat is existential: "We're nothing, you and I. Only triumphs of electronic wizardry, simulectronic shadows!" (1999, 85). In Galouye's story, the realization that one is oneself a synthetic subject results in two sorts of scepticism: scepticism about existence and scepticism about free will. Another troubling thought is that this implies that it may well be that "just as you are manipulating your ID units, there is a greater simulectronicist in a greater world manipulating you—all of us" (1999, 87). As the story unfolds, the mounting evidence leads Hall slowly to the realization that he is himself nothing but a "subjective analog" in another, higher-level total simulation environment. In Galouye's story, it unfortunately transpires that the "Master Simulectronicist" is a sadistic megalomaniac.

On the other hand, were it to be possible to build a machine that can simulate subjects of experience, this, the novel suggests, may also have benefits:

> We have here a surgical instrument that can dissect the very soul itself! It can take a human being apart, motive by motive, instinct by instinct. It can dig to the core of our basic drives, fears, aspirations. It can track down and study, analyze, classify and show us how to do something about every trait that goes into the makeup of any individual. It can explain and uncover the sources of prejudice, bigotry, hate, perverse sentiment. By studying analog beings in a simulated system, we can chart the entire spectrum of human relations. . . . The simulator . . . will show us how to cleanse the mortal spirit of the last vestiges of its animal origins. (Galouye 1999, 72–73)

The very same claim, we should note, is made by Pessoa of his method of metaphysical dreaming: "To reduce sensation to a science, to make psychological analysis into a microscopically precise method—that's the goal that occupies, like a steady thirst, the hub of my life's will" (2002, 431). And, again: "I believe that the future historian of his own sensations may be able to make a precise science out of the attitude he takes towards his self-awareness. We're only in the beginnings of this difficult art—at this point just an art: the chemistry of sensations in its as yet alchemical stage. This scientist of tomorrow will pay special attention to his own inner life, subjecting it to analysis with a precision instrument created out of himself" (2002, #76). Pessoa also speaks of "the slow analysis of sensations, . . . used as an atomic science of the soul" (2002, #155). At first despondent, Hall gathers additional solace from the Cartesian thought that our essence lies in our self-awareness, not the stuff we are made of.

Electronically simulated subjective "reaction units" are not, of themselves, heteronyms. They are like the characters in a novel, units of subjective feeling, perhaps only reluctantly at the mercy of their Author or Operator. Heteronymy does enter the story, however, with the proposal that Hall himself can be lowered into the simulated total environment: as the technician puts it, "I can cut you in on either a direct empathy or personal surveillance circuit" (1999, 41). That is to say, Hall can be given to share the field perspective of one of the subjective analogues through a process of "empathic coupling," or else he can be introduced into the environment as a new entity, as a simulacrum of himself. Hall opts for the first, and

> then I was through, on the other side. And there was that fleeting moment of fear and confusion as my conceptual processes readjusted to the perceptual faculties of D. Thompson—IDU-7412. I sat at the controls of an air van leisurely watching the analog city slip below. I was sensitive even to the steady rise and fall of my (Thompson's) chest and the warmth of the sun that blazed through the plexidome. But it was a passive association. I could only look, listen, feel. I had no motor authority. Nor was there any way the subjective unit could be aware of the empathic coupling. I slipped down to the lower, subvocal level and encountered his flow of conscious thought: I was annoyed that I had fallen behind schedule. But, what the hell, I (IDU-7412) didn't give a damn. Why, I could draw down twice as much with any other vanning firm. Satisfied with the completeness of the coupling I (Doug Hall) pulled back from total perceptive empathy and saw through Thompson's eyes as he glanced at the man in the other seat. (1999, 44)

When the film director Rainer Werner Fassbinder renders this scene in his 1973 film adaptation, *World on a Wire* (Fassbinder 1973), he uses the filmic device of the first-person shot: the audience sees as if through the windshield of the delivery van onto a deserted street. As the philosopher of film Ruggero Eugeni notes, the immersed subject in a first-person shot is an experiential "intermedia figure" and not merely "an entity defined by its position in a specific location" (Eugeni 2012).

The bracketed disambiguations of the first-person pronoun are what indicate that we are now in the realm of heteronymy, so that Doug Hall is able to affirm, "In the simulation, I am IDU-7412." We have a frame of heteronymy, an immersive central position, and something like a way of seeing and feeling. The frame is the electronically simulated arena of experience. The centre is the perspective determined by the position of "reaction unit" IDU-7412. That is, as Galouye clearly understands, not enough for Hall to "be" this subjective analogue in the simulation; as he puts it, it is I (Doug Hall) who merely sees through their eyes. For it to be I (IDU-7412) there also must be "empathic coupling," which Galouye takes to consist in first-personal access to the analogue's thoughts (of earning twice as much) and emotions (of annoyance and not giving a damn). This is, to a first approximation, what a way of experiencing might consist in, especially if we think of empathy as not so much a matter of knowing *what* someone else is feeling as knowing *how*, from the inside, they are feeling. What Galouye's distinction between "empathic coupling" and "seeing through their eyes" aims to capture, then, is something akin to the point I made in Chapter 2 about the excessive austerity in Valberg's conception of immersive centrality, the need to supplement centre with style. Indeed, most philosophical discussions of virtual reality fail to see that there can be virtual subjects as well as virtual objects. They rely exclusively on centre and centrality—that is, on perspectival location. It is as though I simply enter a virtual world, exactly as myself, and while the world is made virtual I remain actual.

Talk of empathy does point towards a problem, however. A Pessoan heteronym is another I of me, and it doesn't have any existence prior to or separate from me (with the caveat that Pessoa returns to the same heteronym, Alberto Caeiro for instance, over and over again, and to that degree is engaging empathically with an already existing persona). In the story, on the other hand, the subjective reaction unit, a "person" within the simulation, already has a full mental life, one into which Doug Hall inserts himself. Are there now, then, two selves in one body? Galouye doesn't want to say that, and instead resorts to the contrivance of having the recipient of "empathic coupling" lose consciousness. This is what happens when Doug Hall is himself a recipient of such coupling. Indeed, it will transpire that Hall is a simulacrum of the Operator himself, and so, in those moments when the Operator empathically couples with Hall, is a heteronym of the Operator within the simulation. "How can the Operator be me and not be me at the same time?" he ponders, in another uncanny echo of Pessoa. "Douglas Hall recreated *himself* as a character in *his* simulator," comes the reply. "You mean I'm exactly like the Operator?" "To a point. The physical resemblance is perfect. But there's been a divergence of psychological traits. I can see now that the Hall up there is a megalomaniac" (Galouye 1999, 148). That's strikingly reminiscent of Pessoa's comment about his semi-heteronym Bernardo Soares, "a semi-heteronym because his personality, although not my own, doesn't differ from my own but is a mere mutilation of it. He's me without my logical reasoning and emotion" (Pessoa 2001, 258–259). And Hall, by now aware that he too is a "subjective analog" in another total environment simulator, reflects on the one whose heteronym he sometimes is, in fact an orthonym, for it transpires that the Operator's name too is "Douglas Hall":

> I considered the Douglas Hall in that upper existence. In a sense, he and I were merely different facets of the same person. . . . He was a person; I was a person. He enjoyed an infinite advantage over me, of course. But beyond that, all that separated us was a simulectronic barrier—a barrier that had perverted his perspective, warped his mind, fed him delusions of grandeur, and turned him into a megalomaniac. He had tortured and murdered ruthlessly, manipulated reactional entities with brutal indifference.

> But, morally, was he guilty of anything? He had taken lives—Fuller's and Collingsworth's. But they had never really existed. Their only reality, their only sense of being, had been the subjective awareness he had imparted to them through the intricate circuitry of his simulator. (Galouye 1999, 156)

David Chalmers argues, in his book about virtual reality, *Reality+*, that virtual reality is genuine reality and that simulated minds are genuine minds. He writes, "Can a digital system be conscious? Or are only humans and animals conscious? The question matters a great deal in thinking about digital worlds. Consider the virtual world of Daniel Galouye's *Simulacron-3*, which pioneered the simulation genre. This virtual world is a pure simulation, containing many simulated humans with simulated brains. Are these simulated humans conscious? If they are, then to shut down the system irreversibly would be an atrocity, a sort of genocide. If they're not conscious, then they are digital zombies, and shutting down the system seems no worse than turning off an ordinary video game" (Chalmers 2022, 276). Galouye has assumed that the answer is in the affirmative, that the subjective reaction units really are conscious, and Chalmers agrees: "Simulated minds are genuine minds" (2022, 292).

I have also taken this for granted. My interest has been in a more specific question about the book, which is what happens when Hall "cuts" himself into that virtual world. Does the notion of "empathic coupling," in which the first-person point of view of one of the simulated minds is assumed by a mind from outside the simulation, make any sense at all? My answer is that Pessoa's concept of heteronymy is exactly what we need to make sense of this notion. "In the simulation," thinks Hall, "I am IDU-7412." This is not the same as Hall uploading himself into the simulation, something that is dubbed by the narrator "being cut in as a personal surveillance circuit," for "since it wasn't an empathy coupling, I wasn't imprisoned in the back of some ID unit's mind. Instead I was *there*—in a pseudo-physical sense" (1999, 59). It would now be as if, as Ashton puts it, "a god dropped down and started talking to you" (1999, 59). Such uploading isn't what we are interested in here; rather, we are interested in the possibility of being, within the simulation, someone else. While Chalmers rightly argues that simulated minds are genuine minds, and that real minds can be uploaded into simulations, the possibility we are discussing takes both for granted. It is the further possibility that a real mind can assume the *bearing* of a simulated mind. As I demonstrated in Chapter 2, that possibility does indeed make sense. To draw on the terminology of that discussion, there is an important distinction to be made between two different ways to be in a simulation, between mere incarnation and full heteronymy.

Avatars and *Avatāras*

The word "avatar" is one of those that has made it across from Sanskrit into English. It did so in the 1980s with video games such as *Ultima IV: Quest of the Avatar*. In gaming jargon, an avatar is a virtual body in a virtual reality, the particular body over which the gamer has executive control; if the game is immersive, it dictates the first-person perspective from which the gamer sees the action unfold. David Chalmers thinks that this is also the original Sanskrit use. He writes:

> The word "avatar" comes from the Hindu tradition, in which it is used for the physical bodies that gods such as Viṣṇu take on when they come down to Earth. Viṣṇu is said to inhabit a physical body with human form—an avatar. The embodiment may be temporary, but while it lasts the avatar is Viṣṇu's body. (2022, 219)

And this, he suggests, is just how it is for virtual avatars too: "In my view, virtual avatars have much the same status as Viṣṇu's physical avatars. I can be embodied in a virtual avatar. The embodiment may be temporary, but when I inhabit an avatar, it's my virtual body" (ibid.). I agree with Chalmers that this is how the term has come to be used in the virtual reality literature, but I am sceptical about his exegesis of its meaning in the Hindu tradition. It is in fact very germane to our discussion of *Simulacron-3* to see how the Sanskrit word *avatāra* is actually employed.

Notice that the idea of an avatar as my virtual body, a body I have executive control over within the simulation, carries with it no implication of heteronymy. It is the same me, the me as on the outside; I simply happen to be embodied virtually in my avatar inside the simulation. When we speak of Matsya as an *avatāra* of Viṣṇu, is that all we mean—that this body, which is half fish and half man, is simply a body Viṣṇu has decided to inhabit during a brief stint on earth? Were Matsya, instead, a heteronym of Viṣṇu, then something more would need to be brought into the picture. It would now be that Viṣṇu is on the earth as Matsya, that there is a way of being on earth for Viṣṇu distinctively associated with his being Matsya. Of course, for that idea to make sense there must be a frame of heteronymy, a context akin to simulation or dreaming, whereas a literal-minded reading of the *avatāra* doctrine simply has it that Viṣṇu has descended to earth.

Let us look more closely to see if an *avatāra* is merely an incarnation or has associations more resembling heteronymy. The term means literally "descent, alighting, descending or going down into" (Apte's dictionary), from the Sanskrit root *tṝ*-, "to pass across, over," with the verbal prefix *ava*-, signifying a movement downwards. The term *avatāra* thus comes to be used as a general expression to designate entities that come down to earth from some higher realm. This fits with the description in *Simulacron-3* of Hall being "cut into" the simulation from, as it were, above. Recall Ashton's words: such a cutting-into would be as if "a god dropped down and started talking to you." And yet the Hindu picture is immediately made more complicated, because a descent is only half of the story.

Following the descent, there is a second step described as a "manifestation" (*prādurbhū-*) or as a "birth" (*jan-*). The idea is there in *Bhagavad-gītā* 4.6–7, which has Kṛṣṇa say, "Although I am unborn and imperishable and the lord of the creatures indeed, I transform the nature that is mine and take birth through an appearance of myself [*ātmamāyā*]. For whenever the moral law languishes, Bhārata, and lawlessness flourishes, I generate myself [*ātmānam sṛjāmi*]." The *Harivaṃśa* 44.80 describes Viṣṇu's descent in similar terms: "Therefore, come personally, O Viṣṇu; let us go [together] on earth. Through yourself create yourself [*visṛjātmānam ātmanā*]." So it is never simply a matter of dropping down; there is also always some sort of self-creation involved.

André Couture has gone further. He has noted that the term *avatāraṇa* has a precise technical use in the language of theatre, where it is used to describe the movement performed by actors as they move from the wings to the stage itself (Couture 2001, 319). As Couture notes in addition, "The facts that, in the *Bhāgavata-purāṇa*, Kṛṣṇa is presented as an actor (10.18.11; 21.5–8; 23.22) and that the Vṛndāvana forest is depicted as a stage upon which he plays his sports (10.5.18) are also entirely consistent with the idea that an *avatāra* is basically a deity who dons various disguises as he takes his place on stage" (Couture 2010, 703). So Viṣṇu is an actor making an entrance, his actions having the form of a play (*līlā*) on a stage. As Couture puts it, "Not only does Viṣṇu descend upon the earth to remove its burden, but he is also an actor who dons the most unexpected disguises" (Couture 2001, 323).

We now have a frame of heteronymy, for the earth is itself a stage, and it is on this stage that Viṣṇu becomes Kṛṣṇa. I would correct one detail in Couture's description. When an actor walks onto the stage, it is not quite right to say that they don a disguise. Rather, what happens is that they move into character; they are no longer themselves but the character whose role it is they play. This movement into character is a heteronymic movement, not fully or properly represented as merely pseudonymous disguise. It is the actor-as-character who now appears, and the audience sees the character in the actor, or, rather, sees the character's emotion in the actor's dramatic performance. Pessoa himself appeals to a dramaturgic analogy: "As a dramatist (without the poet) I automatically transform what I feel into an expression far removed from what I felt, and I create, in my emotions, a nonexistent person who truly felt that feeling and, in feeling it, felt yet other, related emotions that I, purely I, forgot to feel" (Pessoa 2001, 246). The actor Viṣṇu, in character as Kṛṣṇa, has undergone a heteronymic transformation. This is all a far cry from the idea that he is simply a video gamer controlling Kṛṣṇa's body. I wonder if it is a coincidence that here too a forest sets the stage, for Vṛndāvana indeed is a forest of estrangement.

Dreaming has a similar structure. The immersed subject within a dream is not a mere avatar, in the gaming sense, of the dreaming subject, the one whose dream it is. Evan Thompson writes that "the dream ego is like an avatar in a virtual world; the dreaming self is its user. . . . [L]ucidity can enable the dreaming self to act consciously and deliberately in the dream state through the persona of the dream ego, who becomes like an avatar in a role-playing game" (Thompson 2014, 109–110). I think, however, that the subject within the dream is, rather, an *avatāra*, not an avatar, of the dreaming subject, the one who I become within the dream.

While we are on the topic of Sanskrit-English translation, let me note that if we are to seek a Sanskrit translation of "virtual," it is presumably *kṛtrima*. Monier Monier-Williams' dictionary lists as meanings of *kṛtrima* "artificial, made artificially, assumed," and even "simulated." As well as being the term used by grammarians to distinguish technical terms from ordinary words, *kṛtrima* refers, according to the *Śivapurāṇa* 2.3.7, to dolls: "During her childhood, the goddess played frequently with balls and dolls on the sandy banks of the Gaṅgā among her playmates." Meanwhile, Kṛṣṇa in the *Harivaṃśa* 58.42 says of an *avatāra* that "the deities in heaven do not see your self-existing form, they worship only your artificial form [*kṛtrimaṃ rūpam*]" (cited in Couture 2001, 322). Finally, to anticipate our later discussion, Sarasvatī in the *Mokṣopāya* interrogates Līlā as to the distinction between what is natural (*akṛtima*) and what is artificial (*kṛtrima*) (MU 3.18.15; cf. Chakrabarti 2018, 7). The word *kṛtrima* here does not mean "fake," for plenty of things can have both a natural origin and a manufactured origin. Another generator of virtual worlds in India is *māyā*, which is often misleadingly translated as "illusion" (see Chapter 7) but means rather "artistic power" (Doniger 1984, 118, 213). *Māyā* is what generates things that are *kṛtrima*, and therefore "virtual" or "artificial." *Māyā* does not mean "illusion" because what is made by this artistic power is real enough.

Chalmers reads the *avatāra* concept as indicating simply the idea of inhabiting a virtual body, overlooking its heteronymic significance. The same oversight influences his reading of the famous story about the sage Nārada. Nārada, recall, receives from Viṣṇu a lesson about the nature of appearance (*māyā*, artistic power). Viṣṇu has Nārada transform into a woman, and to live as a woman and wife for what seems like many years, years of pleasure followed by suffering, only for Viṣṇu to break the spell of the appearance and return Nārada to his previous state as if nothing had happened. Chalmers comments that "Nārada's life as Suśilā is akin to life in a virtual world—a simulation with Viṣṇu acting as the simulator" (2022, 7). So far so good. But he goes on to add:

> Suśilā's body was akin to a virtual body, in a virtual world generated by Viṣṇu rather than by a computer. It was the body that Suśilā perceived with, acted with, presented, and identified with. I think that just as Viṣṇu genuinely had an earthly body during his periods of embodiment as an avatar, Suśilā genuinely had a female virtual body during her life as a woman. (2022, 223)

Chalmers wants to say that in the Viṣṇu-generated virtual reality, Nārada has the virtual body of Suśilā. He recognizes, though, that more is going on than that, and so refers to the virtual body as Suśilā's, not as Nārada's. For it is not merely the case, in this story, that Nārada is incarnated as a woman. Rather, what we must say is that in the Viṣṇu-generated simulation, Nārada is Suśilā. And that is just to say that Suśilā is a heteronym of Nārada. The actual wording of the story makes the point clear: "Viṣṇu took me to a beautiful pond and invited me to bathe in it. I entered the pool as Viṣṇu watched me, and in it I left my male form and became a woman. Viṣṇu picked up my lute and went away, and I forgot all about my former body. . . . For twelve years that passed like a single moment, I forgot my former body and former life as a sage. . . . Sometimes I was happy, sometimes saddened. . . . As I lamented [the death of my sons], Viṣṇu took the form of a Brahmin and came to me and said, 'Why are you so sad? This is just a mistake [*bhrama*] and a delusion [*moha*]. Who are you, and whose sons are these?" (Doniger 1984, 82). Evidently, it is not simply the case that Nārada is perceiving the world in the body of Suśilā, simply exhibiting the perceptual, volitional, and affective centrality discussed by Valberg and hinted at by Chalmers. It is rather that his entire way of being, his mode of experience, is now as Suśilā. So it is not a story about incarnation, of being in a virtual body, but a tale of *bearing*, becoming another I within a frame of heteronymy.

None of this is to deny that one can find examples of simple incarnation in the Indian texts, cases where what is simulated is myself inhabiting a virtual body, and nothing more. A late retelling of the Lavaṇa story, for instance, transforms it into a rather straightforward story about "people entering another body" (Doniger 1984, 168). Often, in the Indian texts, it is a god who induces in a human being a simulated field of experience. Viṣṇu, Sarasvatī, and the rest are fond of teaching us lessons about the nature of reality by having us drop into virtual environments. There are Buddhists too who speak about a "body in the dream" (*svapnāntika-śarīra*), by which they mean the body of the immersed subject within the dream, and they treat it as real. For otherwise, argues the Buddhist philosopher Prajñākaragupta, "how could you explain the fact that when the dream body is beaten, the dreamer feels afraid? It is never the case that one person eats an oily cake and another dies of thirst" (Hayashi 2001, 566). In reply to an opponent who objects that "a body in a dream is fake," Prajñākaragupta says that "this is not correct because it is accepted that such a body has the ability to produce an effect" (Hayashi 2001, 568, citing Prajñākaragupta's commentary on the *Pramāṇavārttika*).

We don't need to dig so deeply, though, for closer at hand there is already the famous explanation offered by Kṛṣṇa in the *Bhagavad-gītā* 2.22 of reincarnation as akin to donning a fresh set of clothes:

> As a man discards his worn-out clothes
> And puts on different ones that are new.
> So the one in the body discards aged bodies
> And joins with other ones that are new. (van Buitenen 1981, 76–77)

This is a simple formulation of mere bodily immersion. Henry Miller would later provide a twist on the theme: "My body is heavy as lead when I throw it into bed. I pass immediately into the lowest depth of dream. This body, which has become a sarcophagus with stone handles, lies perfectly motionless; the dreamer rises out of it, like a vapor, to circumnavigate the world. The dreamer seeks vainly to find a form and shape that will fit his ethereal essence. Like a celestial tailor, he tries on one body after another, but they are all misfits. Finally he is obliged to return to his own body, to reassume the leaden mould, to become a prisoner of the flesh, to carry on in torpor, pain and ennui" (Miller 1965, 13–14). This Cartesian fantasy, however, is about as far removed from Pessoan heteronymic plurality as it is possible to be.

4

A Life Lived in Serial, and in Parallel

Being plural like the universe means, for Fernando Pessoa, two very different things at the same time. One is to live one's life as a series of heteronyms, a sequence of virtual selves or "individuated points of view" (Zenith 2021, xxix), each with its own style of being in the world, a style that is associated with those affective modes of poetic attention Pessoa identifies as astonishment and admiration. The other, even more radical idea, which seems to predate the invention of heteronymy, consists in the thought that one might lead multiple lives in parallel, meaning specifically that one occupies simultaneously a plurality of first-person positions. Neither idea is easy; indeed, they can seem to teeter on the brink of unintelligibility. And yet, as I will show in this chapter, both ideas, remarkably enough, have been foreseen in the literature of classical India.

Rudra and the Makropulos Case

In *Simulacron-3*, the protagonist, Doug Hall, wonders, in effect, why anyone would heteronymize themselves. "Why do you suppose he did it?" he asks about the Operator, who had created a simulacrum of himself within his simulation, Doug Hall himself. "I couldn't even guess at first. But now I know. It has to do with unconscious motivation. A sort of Dorian Gray effect" (Galouye 1999, 148). Pessoa had the habit of killing off his heteronyms, but in other hands might not heteronymy be a vehicle for a form of life extension? I have in mind a play, written by Karel Čapek and first performed in 1922, called *The Makropulos Case*. This play

Fernando Pessoa. Jonardon Ganeri, Oxford University Press. © Oxford University Press 2024.
DOI: 10.1093/oso/9780197636688.003.0005

has become well known to philosophers thanks to an essay by Bernard Williams. For Williams, the philosophical interest of the play lies in the idea that immortality, were it even to be available, would not be desirable; indeed, it would be decidedly tedious. The play's protagonist, Elina Makropulos, was given an elixir of life by her father, a sixteenth-century court physician, but by the time she has reached the age of 342 she has had enough. She has been forty-two for the last three hundred years and is bored, a boredom, as Williams puts it, "connected with the fact that everything that could happen and make sense to one particular human being of 42 had already happened to her" (1973, 90). By now she is known under the name Emilia Marty, and confesses to the fact that before this she was Ellian MacGregor and Eugenia Montez and Elsa Müller and Ekaterina Myshkin. Each of these names is linked with a different period in the life of the eternal forty-two-year-old heroine. Are these names merely pseudonyms of the same person, or are they designations of a succession of ways of being in the world at different times—that is, different heteronyms? Williams writes:

> There are difficult questions, if one presses the issue, about [her] constancy of character. How is this accumulation of memories related to this character which she eternally has, and to the character of her existence? Are they much the same kind of events repeated? Then it is itself strange that she allows them to be repeated, accepting the same repetitions, the same limitations—indeed, *accepting* is what it later becomes, when earlier it would not, or even could not, have been that. The repeated patterns of personal relations, for instance, must take on a character of being inescapable. Or is the pattern of her experiences not repetitious in this way, but varied? Then the problem shifts, to the relation between these varied experiences, and the fixed character: how can it remain fixed, through an endless series of very various experiences? The experiences must surely happen to her without

really affecting her; she must be, as EM is, detached and withdrawn. (1973, 90)

Williams argues that it is desirable to extend one's life indefinitely only if two conditions are met. The first condition is that "it should clearly be *me* who lives for ever." The second condition is that "the state in which I survive should be one which, to me looking forward, will be adequately related, in the life it presents, to those aims which I now have in wanting to survive at all" (1973, 91). He considers that the most tempting alternative to EM's life of immortal boredom is "survival by means of an indefinite series of lives"—the "serial and disjoint lives" alternative, as he also calls it. Yet all "versions of this belief which have actually existed have immediately failed the first condition: they get nowhere near providing any consideration to mark the difference between rebirth and new birth" (1973, 92).

Perhaps we can derive from Pessoa's theory of heteronyms a new solution. For let us imagine that each of the lives in the indefinite series is related to the one that came immediately before it by the relation of heteronymy. That is to say, there is a heteronymic chain, a nested series of heteronyms. If the suggestion is intelligible, then, I think, a life as a heteronymic chain of lives will meet both of Williams' conditions. As regards the first condition, it is built into the very notion of a heteronym that my heteronym is *me* again, and I showed in detail in Chapter 2 how to make good that claim. What the second condition will now amount to is the requirement that as I anticipate life as my heteronym, that life is one that satisfies my present desire to go on living. And surely this is the case, if indeed the newness of a new way of being in the world is associated, as Pessoa claims it is, with astonishment and admiration, even for the most mundane and familiar of things.

EM's problem from this perspective is that the series of "EM"s is actually a series of pseudonyms and not a series of heteronyms: her character remains constant and only her name changes. Had it been instead the case that her life was as a series of heteronyms, then her immortal boredom never would have arisen, because even if she were continuously experiencing the same things or sorts of things, she would endlessly experience them in ever renewed ways. "There is for me—there was—a wealth of meaning in a thing so ridiculous as a door-key; a nail on a wall; a cat's whiskers," says Pessoa. I will postpone until the last section of this chapter a more thorough analysis of Pessoa's views about death, the afterlife, and immortality, but suffice it to say here that he does not find the prospect tedious: "Yes, tomorrow or when Fate decides, the one in me who pretended to be I will come to an end" (2002, 279).

The idea of a life consisting in a heteronymic chain of lives is, remarkably, foreseen in a story from a classical Sanskrit treatise, the *Mokṣopāya*. It is the story of a hundred Rudras:

> Once upon a time there was a monk who was inclined to imagine things rather a lot. He would meditate and study all the time, and fast for days on end. One day, this fancy came to him: "Just for fun, I will experience what happens to ordinary people." As soon as he had this idea, his thought somehow took the form of another man [*sañcintya ceto 'sya sthitaṃ kiñcin narāntaram*; 6.66.6], and that man wished for an identity and a name, even though he was just made of thought [*tena cittanareṇātha kṛtaṃ nāmātmanīcchayā*; 6.66.7]. And by pure accident, as when a crow happens to be under a tree when a palm fruit falls from it and hits him, he thought, "I am Jīvaṭa" [*jīvaṭo 'smīti*; 6.66.7]. This dream man [*svapnapuruṣa*; 6.66.8], Jīvaṭa, enjoyed himself for a long time in a town made in a dream. There he drank too much and fell into a heavy sleep, and in his dream he saw himself as a Brahmin who read all day long. One day, that Brahmin fell asleep, worn out from the day's work, but those daily activities were still alive within him, like a tree inside a seed, and so he saw himself, in a dream, as a prince [*apaśyat svayaṃ svapne sāmantatvam*; 6.66.12]. One day that prince fell asleep after a heavy meal, and in his dream he saw himself as a king who ruled many lands and

indulged in every sort of luxury. One day that king fell asleep, having gorged himself on his every desire, and in his dream he saw himself as a celestial woman. That woman fell into a deep sleep in the languor that followed making love, and she saw herself as a doe with darting eyes. That doe one day fell asleep and dreamed that she was a clinging vine, because she had been accustomed to eating vines; for animals dream, too, and they always remember what they have seen and heard.

The vine saw herself as a bee that used to buzz among the vines; the bee fell in love with a lotus in a lotus pond and one day became so intoxicated by the lotus sap he drank that his wits became numb; and just then an elephant came to that pond and trampled the lotus, and the bee, still attached to the lotus, was crushed with it on the elephant's tusk. As the bee looked at the elephant, he saw himself as an elephant in rut. That elephant in rut fell into a deep pit and became the favourite elephant of a king. One day the elephant was cut to pieces by a sword in battle, and as he went to his final resting place he saw a swarm of bees hovering over the sweet ichor that oozed from his temples, and so the elephant became a bee again. The bee returned to the lotus pond and was trampled under the foot of an elephant, and just then he noticed a goose beside him in the pond, and so he became a goose. That goose moved through other births, other wombs, for a long time, until one day, when he was a goose in a flock of other geese, he realized that, being a goose, he was the same as the swan of Brahmā, the Creator. Just as he had this thought, he was shot by a hunter and he died, and then he was born as the swan of Brahmā.

One day the swan saw the god Rudra, and he thought, with sudden certainty, "I am Rudra" [*rudro 'ham*; 6.67.2]. Immediately that idea was reflected like an image in a mirror, and he took on the form of Rudra. This Rudra indulged in every pleasure that entered his mind, living in the palace of Rudra and attended by Rudra's servants. . . . At the end of the round of a hundred rebirths is Rudra, and I am Rudra, I am he [*rudras so 'yam ahaṃ sthitaḥ*;

> 6.67.21], the one who stands in the flux of rebirths where everyone is fooled by his own mind. (MU 6.66.1–67.21; Doniger 1984, 207–209)

Rāma wonders how Jīvaṭa, the brahmin, the swan, and the sage, if they were all parts of the monk's dream, could be real (*para*; 6.68.1). Vasiṣṭha explains that it is by focusing the mind on the wish "May I be a wise person" or "May I be a divine" that one makes oneself one or one hundred, an idiot or a pandit, a god or a human being (*iha vidyādharo 'haṃ syām iha syām aham eḍikā / ity ekadhyānasāphalyadṛṣṭānto 'syāṃ kriyāsthitau // ekatvaṃ ca śatatvaṃ ca maurkhyaṃ pāṇḍityam eva ca / devatvaṃ mānuṣatvaṃ ca deśakālakriyākramaiḥ* [MU 6.68.24–25]). The leading role in the process is given to singly focused attention (*eka-dhyāna*). The formula used to describe the various transformations, "In the dream, he saw himself as X" or "In the dream, he saw himself being X" (*apaśyat svayaṃ svapne X-tvam*), clearly indicates that what is in play is a phenomenon of heteronymic immersion, just as we saw it illustrated in Pessoa's description of seeing himself as a fly. Zeno Vendler writes, in a similar vein, of what he calls the performance of "intersubjective transference in imagination":

> What I am now called upon to do, or try to do, is to imagine the cat's pain: what it must be like, not for me but for the cat, to be in that situation. . . . I have to imagine being that subject to be able to imagine that pain: what it must feel like being on the floor, with a small furry body, and a tail stepped upon by a huge and hefty creature. (Vendler 1984, 7; cf. 33)

Intersubjective transference in imagination is just another name for heteronymy.

The story is again discussed later in the text, Rāma asking, "What became of the hundred Rudras? Were they all Rudras, or weren't they? And how could a hundred minds be made from a single mind [*ekasmād bhagavaṃś cittāt kathaṃ cittaśataṃ kṛtam*; 6.73.4]?" Vasiṣṭha is adamant that "all the forms in the dream were, in fact, Rudra, a hundred-fold Rudra" (MU 6.73.3; Doniger 1984, 212). Rudra's life, whatever its drawbacks, could never be said to be boring, if it is to live in serial the life of a king, a brahmin, a celestial woman, a doe, a bee, an elephant, a goose, a swan, and many, many more. It is, incidentally, fascinating to discover in this story an echo of the famous story of the dream of the butterfly from the *Zhuangzi*, where Zhuangzi dreams of being a butterfly and a butterfly dreams of being Zhuangzi (for a Pessoan interpretation of Zhuangzi's parable, see Ganeri 2021, 124–129). In our story, Rudra dreams of being a bee who dreams of being an elephant who dreams of being a bee.

Mark Johnston has defended an interesting view about survival and personal identity that has some points of commonality with the one currently under discussion. He argues that persons are Protean, that "as with Proteus, who could assume the forms of a lion, a leopard, a serpent, or a pig, our essence could allow changes in our form of embodiment," as long as any such change is "not at odds with the person's identity-determining dispositions" (Johnston 2010, 283–284). (Recall how Borges described Shakespeare as a Protean poet.) Was Elina Makropulos a Protean person? In a sense, yes, because her "identity-determining dispositions" remained the same throughout, and that, indeed, was the source of her tedium. The only difference is that her body did not age, and she had no need to resort to the Protean expedient recommended in *Bhagavad-gītā* 2.22: "As leaving aside worn-out garments / A man takes other, new ones, / So leaving aside worn-out bodies, / To other new ones goes the embodied." Yet Johnston's notion of an identity-determining disposition is looser than that of a fixed character; he defines it as a disposition "to somehow deeply and consistently identify with some future person," a disposition one can have "even if that disposition is not essentially dependent on that person's continuing to exemplify your present personality" (Johnston 2010, 275–276).

How, though are you meant now to be able to "deeply and consistently" identify with a future person whose personality is a mystery to you? Pessoa does indeed identify with his heteronyms, but that is because, as their creator, the personality of his heteronyms is epistemically transparent to him.

Richard Wollheim is the only philosopher I know of to anticipate an idea similar to what I am calling heteronymic chains, and the possibility of living a life consisting in one. He refers to a case where I "set myself to centrally imagine John's centrally imagining Angus's centrally imagining Stephen's writing his diary," but rejects it on the grounds that

> no matter how much I know about these three friends, no matter how successfully I can speculate about John's understanding of Angus's beliefs about what Stephen thinks worth putting into his diary, I am certain not to have this information in a form in which it would be available for me to use appropriately as the narrative unfolds. Multiply embedded repertoires are not accessible, and that is one powerful reason why such repertoires are in effect nominal. (Wollheim 1984, 79)

Putting the argument in my terminology, what Wollheim claims is that heteronymic chaining would constitute survival only if the individual at any link in the chain has access to the inner life of every subsequent link. Recall, however, Williams' second condition. What it states is that the state in which I survive "should be one which, to me looking forward, will be adequately related, in the life it presents, to those aims which I now have in wanting to survive at all" (Williams 1973, 91). It is sufficient to meet this condition that the individual can anticipate the life of their immediate successor in the heteronymic chain (i.e., their heteronym), perhaps together with the knowledge that this is true of heteronyms in general. Heteronymy is not transitive, and survival by heteronymic chaining does not require the sort of omniscience about my future Wollheim would impose upon it. It is true, as Derek Parfit says, that in the question of one's survival, "personal identity is not what matters. What matters is relation R: psychological connectedness and/or continuity with the right kind of cause" (Parfit 1984, 215). What we have is a new proposal as to the content of relation R, that relation R is the relation of heteronymy. This will not, of course, be any sort of reductionist account of persons, because it will not be true that "a complete description could be impersonal" (Parfit 1984, 212), and survival will still require bodily preservation or exchange.

One Life Lived in Parallel?

Is it even conceivable, let alone possible, that one might live multiple lives in parallel, by which I mean that one is, simultaneously, an occupant of many first-person perspectives? In *The Book of Disquiet*, thanks to the presence of his female other in the forest of enchantment, the admiration and astonishment of the protagonist are fused with a strange sort of love, which is only partly romantic: "I, I, unsure of which one I was, or if I was both, or neither" (Pessoa 2002, #386), he says, in a strange echo of Nāgārjuna's tetralemmic logic. The introduction of this female double into the story serves two ends. One is certainly to provide for a peculiar form of astonishment in this strange forest, a delight in sharing the experience without quite being certain if one is sharing it. But it is also an anticipation of a theme that would continue to occupy Pessoa as he worked on *The Book of Disquiet*, the theme of a single life lived in parallel:

> To dream, for example, that I'm simultaneously, separately, severally the man and the woman on a stroll that a man and a woman are taking along the river. (2002, #157)

> It would be interesting to be two kings at the same time: not the one soul of them both, but two distinct, kingly souls. (2002, #404)

> The highest stage of dreaming is when, having created a picture with various figures whose lives we live all at the same time, we are jointly and interactively all of those souls. This leads to an incredible degree of depersonalization and the reduction of our spirit to ashes. (2002, 405)

> And as I pass by those houses, villas, and chalets, I also live the daily lives of all their inhabitants, living them all at the same time. I'm the father, mother, sons, cousins, the maid and the maid's cousins, all together and all at once, thanks to my special talent for simultaneously feeling various and sundry sensations, for simultaneously living the lives of various people—both on the outside, seeing them, and on the inside, feeling them. (2002, #299).

Notice here, in particular, Pessoa's use of the phrase "on the inside, feeling them"—it is more than evident that he is talking about a *de se* imagining, specifically imagining being someone else. Pessoa's astounding thought experiment lends to his philosophy its radically anti-Cartesian outlook, and it is evidently an idea to which Pessoa was committed from the time of his earliest writings.

There is a retelling of the Nārada story that has Viṣṇu say, "I myself am Rādhā when I have the form of a woman, and I am Kṛṣṇa when I have the form of a man. There is, truly, no difference between the two of us, Nārada. This is the secret of Vṛndā" (Doniger 1984, 83). Viṣṇu regrettably doesn't comment on the fact that it is often the case that Rādhā and Kṛṣṇa are present together at the same time. And yet that is just how it is for Pessoa in the forest of enchantment. In fact, there is the faintest of hints of exactly such a situation in the great Indian epic the *Mahābhārata*. Draupadī finds herself in a tight spot, having inadvertently agreed to marry all five of the Pāṇḍava brothers in a single ceremony. Her father, Draupada, is worried about the moral propriety of her situation. He consults the narrator, Vyāsa, who takes him aside and explains in secret that each of the brothers is in fact Indra:

> Vyāsa tells Drupada how the gods once performed a sacrifice in the Naimisa forest. Yama was busy in his sacrificial duties, with the result that creatures no longer died. The gods complained to Brahma that nothing now distinguished them from men; Brahma reassured them that once their rite was completed men would start to die again. As the gods returned to their sacrifice, Indra saw a woman weeping into the Gaṅgā: each of her tears became a golden lotus. When he asked her who she was and why she was weeping, she told him to follow her; he did so, and saw a youth playing dice with some young women. The youth ignored him; Indra began to bluster angrily, but at a glance from the youth he found himself paralysed. Next the youth, who was Śiva, told the woman to bring him close so that he could be divested of his pride, and at her touch he collapsed to the ground. Now he was commanded to remove the summit of the mountain and enter, and whẹn he did so he found four other Indras imprisoned there. When Indra begged for his freedom, Śiva told him that all five Indras would return to their own world only after being born as men. However, he agreed to their stipulation that in their human form they must be begotten by deities: Dharma, Wind, Indra and the Aśvins. He also promised that the goddess Śrī would take human form as their wife. Nārayaṇa agreed to this arrangement, and plucked from his head one white and one black hair: these entered the wombs of Rohiṇī and Devakī, and from them were born Balarāma and Kṛṣṇa.— Vyāsa explains to Drupada that the Pāṇdavas are the five Indras, and Draupadī is Śrī. (Mbh. 1.189ff.; synopsis in Smith 2009)

Vyāsa doesn't quite go as far as to say that all five brothers are identical to Indra: he tells a story in which there are five Indras, alike in qualities. Indeed, it is only here, in this story whispered in secret, that we learn of the five Indras. One might read the story simply as suggesting that the marriage is legitimate because it has a divine sanction, being a reflection on earth of an arrangement the gods themselves find acceptable. But I think the fact that all five Indras are called "Indra," together with the fact that this is the only reference in the epic to there being more than one Indra, supports a different interpretation—namely, that all five Pāṇḍava brothers are heteronyms of Indra, living lives in parallel. *The* Indra promises to use his strength to make a man, the fifth of the brothers (*vīryeṇāhaṃ puruṣaṃ kāryahetor; dadyām eṣāṃ pañcamaṃ matprasūtam*; 1.189). This recalls the second phase in the *avatāra* process, the phase involving self-creation or manifestation. Draupadī has, in effect, simply married the same man five times over, not five different men. If that is so, then the epic has the form, "In the story of the *Mahābhārata*, Indra is Yudhiṣṭhira and Indra is Arjuna and Indra is Bhīma and Indra is Nakula and Indra is Sahadeva." Here too there is a forest, to which Draupadī is banished along with her five husbands—a "forest of estrangement" in more senses than one. In Pessoa's forest of estrangement, Pessoa is both the man and the woman. She is not him and he is not her; their relationship is one of heteronymic community: "We were obscurely two, neither of us knowing for sure if we weren't actually the other, if the uncertain other lived" (Pessoa 2002, 420). Richard Zenith comments that "two selves in one, male and female, Pessoa's narrative . . . sums up the languorous nondrama of self-othered existence" (2021, 364). The most extreme case of all, of course, would be that of *brahman*, who becomes—heteronymically—identical to each and every individual subject of experience (*ātman*) (see Chapter 8 and Ganeri 2021, 138–148).

Yet another refraction of the idea of a life lived in parallel can be retrieved from what we know of the Mesoamerican philosophy of the Maya. Alexus McLeod has explicated the Maya concept of *k'ex*, "substitution," in terms of a notion of *embedded identity*. He writes:

> Janaab Pakal, at his tomb at Palenque, is depicted in the Temple of the Inscriptions at the side as the maize god, signifying rebirth, and is adorned with the Chac Xib Chaak ornament. . . . Pectoral adornment in Maya imagery generally represented the essence of the person depicted. . . . This act is often called *substitution* (*k'ex*). . . . Substitution was thought of as a method of one entity's taking on the essence of another, and in this becoming the being represented. One did not, however, lose one's individual essence in taking on or becoming part of the substituted entity. This is the sense in which we might call the identity of one being with a substitute an *embedded identity*. A ruler, such as Janaab Pakal of Palenque, can become or represent Chack Xib Chaak through substitution, while still remaining Janaab Pakal. At the time of substitution, Janaab Pakal is Janaab Pakal and Chack Xib Chaak. (McLeod 2018, 148)

McLeod notes that "the question then becomes how do we think of entities/persons such as Chack Xib Chaak. One way of thinking of them is as collective persons—a single person made up of a collectivity of essences, perhaps related to the Palenque rulership lineage. Further features of *k'ex* (substitution) can help us here, to understand how the individual and collective essences are related" (2018, 148). Robert Carlsen observes in a similar vein that *k'ex* "relates to what might be best described as a form of reincarnation, an integral aspect of Maya religion . . . *K'ex* is a process of making the new out of the old. At the same time, just as a single plant produces multiple offspring, *k'ex* is change from one into many. Together *jal* and *k'ex* form a concentric system of change within change, a single system of transformation and renewal" (1997, 50–51).

All this very closely mirrors the secret story of the genesis of the five Pāṇḍava brothers, revealed to Draupadī on her wedding night so as to reconcile her father's conscience with her polyandry. Indra has become, through substitution, each of the five. McLeod introduces the helpful notion of an "embedded identity" in order to grasp the sense in which Janaab Pakal is Janaab Pakal and Chack Xib Chaak. The identity of Chack Xib Chaak is embedded within that of Janaab Pakal, not a replacement of it. I think that heteronymy is just the concept we need here to make sense of this notion of embedded identity: within the frame that is constituted by the "concentric system of change," Chack Xib Chaak is Janaab Pakal, and is also all of the other rulers in the Palenque lineage. It would be inaccurate to say that Janaab Pakal literally becomes Chack Xib Chaak; rather, it is within a heteronymous frame of ritual and representation that the identity holds good, just as it makes sense to say, "In my dream, I was X."

The fact that there exist such precursors of the idea that one can live a life in parallel is not, in itself, a defence of the intelligibility of that idea. But it is enough to encourage the thought that such a defence might be available, that this is not merely an idiosyncratic element in Pessoa's philosophy of self. Indeed, I have attempted a philosophical defence of the idea elsewhere, drawing on Pessoa's "intersectionism" (see Ganeri 2021, 33–40).

Death as Deletion

According to Richard Zenith, "Degeneration in the broadest sense—including physical, mental, and societal decadence, personal and collective ruin, and death in all its forms—was foundational to Pessoa's view of how the world and everything in it worked" (Zenith 2021, 236). In *The Book of Disquiet* Fernando Pessoa reflects and reflects again on the phenomenology of death, immortality, and the beyond:

> And then I wonder what this thing is that we call death. I don't mean the mystery of death, which I can't begin to fathom, but the physical sensation of ceasing to live. Humanity is afraid of death, but indecisively. The normal man . . . rarely looks with horror at

> the abyss of nothing. . . . And nothing is less worthy of a thinking man than to see death as a slumber. Why a slumber, if death doesn't resemble sleep? Basic to sleep is the fact that we wake up from it, as we presumably do not from death. . . . Death doesn't resemble slumber, I said, since in slumber one is alive and sleeping, and I don't know how death can resemble anything at all for us, since we have no experience of it, nor anything to compare it to. (2002, #40)

To think of death as sleep is to imagine it as a state that continues even though the door on life has been shut, and that, Pessoa exactly observes, is a mistake. We should not extrapolate in that way from the known to the unknown: "We generally colour our ideas of the unknown with our notions of the known. If we call death a sleep, it's because it seems like a sleep on the outside; if we call death a new life, it's because it seems like something different from life" (2002, #66).

As for the phenomenology of dying, death manifests itself in life as absence, and Pessoa brilliantly expands on the theme:

> Whoever lives like me doesn't die: he terminates, wilts, dries up. The place where he was remains without him being there; the street where he walked remains without him being seen on it; the house where he lived is inhabited by not-him. That's all, and we call it nothing. (2002, #42)

This then is how to imagine the beyond: we imagine the world exactly as we know it, but airbrush ourselves out of the picture. There is an imagined absence in the imagined scene, and that is what it is to imagine one's nonexistence, rather than a blackness or a dream, or any other state in which some semblance of subjectivity or first-personal perspective is maintained. To imagine being dead is to imagine the world from what Thomas Nagel famously called "the view from nowhere." And thus immortality is an illusion. As Pessoa puts it, “How vain is all our striving to create, under the spell of the illusion of not dying!” (2002, 412).

There is, though, another thought in Pessoa, and a more complicated one. It is the idea that in death we are more real than we are in life. It is not death that should be likened to sleep but life itself: “What we call life is the slumber of our real life, the death of what we really are. . . . We’re dead when we think we’re living; we start living when we die” (2002, #178). Pessoa recognises, and even embraces, the paradox and absurdity of the thought: “I’ve always felt that virtue lay in obtaining what was out of one’s reach, in living where one isn’t, in being more alive after death than during life, in achieving something impossible, something absurd, in overcoming—like an obstacle—the world’s very reality” (2002, #145). The impossible act is to imagine one’s life as an “interlude” between one death and another: “Life is thus an interval, a link, a relation, but a relation between what has passed and what will pass, a dead interval between Death and Death” (2002, 412). “Whatever be this interlude played out under the spotlight of the sun and the spangles of the stars, surely there’s no harm in knowing it’s an interlude” (2002, #348). “[M]y salvation lay in interspaces of unconsciousness” (2002, 463). Pessoa offers us one clue as to what he means in saying that death is more real than life. It has to do with the fact, already noted, that death is a “view from nowhere”: “Since every noble soul desires to live life in its entirety—experiencing all things, all places and all feelings—and since this is objectively impossible, the only way for a noble soul to live life is subjectively; only by denying life can it be lived in its totality” (2002, #232). The highest ideal in life is to experience everything from every point of view, which is in effect to inhabit simultaneously every subjective existence. If that is impossible, then the next best thing is not to experience anything at all, since what the two states have in common is the refusal to be imprisoned within a single subjective stance. Forced to occupy a single first-person perspective, we are as if imprisoned on the surface of life, hoping for an immortality that lies in seeing the world without ourselves in it.

It is a mistake to think we know something about those regions of our mind to which we do not actively attend, based on merely an extrapolation from our attentive states, just as it is a mistake to think we can know the state of the unseen light from its state when we actively attend to it. Julian Jaynes put it like this: "Consciousness is a much smaller part of our mental life than we are conscious of, because we cannot be conscious of what we are not conscious of. . . . It is like asking a flashlight in a dark room to search around for something that doesn't have any light shining on it. The flashlight, since there is light in whatever direction it turns, would have to conclude that there is light everywhere. And so consciousness can seem to pervade all mentality when actually it does not" (Jaynes 1976, 23). Similarly, from the fact that for as long as we are alive we are conscious of being so, it does not follow that there is a similar consciousness even when we are no longer alive. One of the most frequently recurring themes in Pessoa is that we must show some respect for the unknowable, for it is the framing narrative that gives meaning to the more mundane narrative of our actual lives, consisting in what is indeed known, experienced, or seen. We do not know "what is beyond the theatre doors," whether it is even life or death (2002, #348). This is the source of the absurdity of life—our impossible desire to know what we know to be unknowable: "Let's absurdify life, from east to west," he says (2002, #372). For Pessoa it is the absurd endeavour to be conscious of unconsciousness: "The consciousness of life's unconsciousness is the oldest tax levied on the intelligence" (2002, #68). "That's all, and we call it nothing; but not even this tragedy of negation can be staged to applause, for we don't even know for sure if it's nothing" (2002, #42). "Let us affirm—and grasp, which would be impossible—that we are conscious of not being conscious, and that we are not what we are" (2002, #413).

Of these absurd attempts to be conscious of that which one is, by definition, not conscious, the absurdity of which one fully understands, the attempts to imagine the afterlife and to imagine being all subjectivity at once are the supreme examples. Yet it is just this absurdity that manifests itself in the very character of our longings, which are, Pessoa says, "half-tones of the soul's consciousness":

> The feelings that hurt most, the emotions that sting most, are those that are absurd: the longing for impossible things, precisely because they are impossible. . . . All these half-tones of the soul's consciousness create in us a painful landscape, an eternal sunset of what we are. (2002, #196)

"To realize a dream," he writes, "one must forget it, tearing away his attention from it. To realize is thus to not realize. Life is full of paradoxes, as roses are of thorns" (2002, #322). So the strange, dreamlike quality of the lives we lead, and their inherent absurdity, comes about as a result of our incessant longing, as it were, to attend to the unattended region in the visual field, to see it as unattended, to render central the peripherality of vision. We know we can do this precisely only by not directing our attention there, and so the only way to realize our longing is by noting the tangential and ethereal effects it has on what is held in view. The staged play is the place on which attention falls, but what we dream of is the interlude. Exactly so too with our desire to know the afterlife, something in principle unknowable because it is defined as the absence of our consciousness. This absurd longing shows up instead in "the half-tones of the soul's consciousness" while we are alive, and is the source of our most intense emotions.

Pessoa comments on something I'm sure we have all experienced—coming across some of our old writings and reading them with a dreadful sense of both alienation and familiarity:

> In this case there's something besides the flow of personality between its own banks: there's an absolute other, an extraneous self

> that was me. . . . It's as if I'd found an old picture that I know is of me, with a different height and with features I don't recognize, but that is undoubtedly me, terrifyingly I. (2002, #188)

I do not *recognize* myself at such times, in the sense of using some features of the presented self in order to identify it as me. Indeed, I barely acknowledge myself in those old writings at all. And yet I know that it is me, and the combination of absolute familiarity and total alienation is indeed terrifying. I wonder if this could be the death experience—a taste of alienation, of distancing, of knowing that whatever it was or will be, it is no longer I. I relive the past but relive it with a sense that I am already traveling in foreign lands. This is the way the afterlife has an effect on the living, because, as Pessoa says, "sometimes the best way to see an object is to delete it, because it subsists in a way I can't quite explain, consisting of the substance of its negation and deletion; this is what I do with vast areas of my real-life being, which, after they're deleted from my picture of myself, transfigure my true being, the one that's real for me" (2002, 434).

PART III

MAKE-BELIEVE AND THE *MOKṢOPĀYA*

5

Reality++

Fernando Pessoa dreams himself Alberto Caeiro. He imagines being Alberto Caeiro, and he becomes Alberto Caeiro *in his dream*. Viṣṇu casts a spell on Nārada, who finds himself as a woman. He lives as that woman for as long as he remains *under the spell*. Hall is "cut" into the total environment simulation on an empathy coupling circuit. Within the simulation, he is IDU-7412, not just seeing the environment from the point of view of the delivery driver but feeling and thinking the way he does. So far in this book I have been exploring the meaning of *entrance* into a simulation: the different forms it might take, and what becomes of *me*. But there is always, or at least often, also an *exit*, and it is time to reflect on the nature of the protagonist's return. Does my emergence simply return me to my former state, or does the experience leave me changed in some fundamental respect? Is it correct even to speak of a return? In the case of Pessoa, it seems more natural to couch the process in terms of *exchange*, the replacement of one heteronym by another, ad infinitum—or, anyway, until he "terminates, wilts, dries up," as he himself puts it (Pessoa 2002, #42). Finally, what is the correct way to think about the relationship between different reality environments? It is hard to resist the temptation to think about them in terms of levels, and of the movement between them as one of descent and ascent. But that might be a mistake: perhaps it is better to picture reality rather as a single space divided into a plurality of regions, so that entrance and return is more akin to crossing a threshold or going through a door than to descending and ascending a floor.

Fernando Pessoa. Jonardon Ganeri, Oxford University Press. © Oxford University Press 2024.
DOI: 10.1093/oso/9780197636688.003.0006

Vasiṣṭha's Argument

These themes are nowhere in literature explored in more detail and with greater sophistication than in the *Mokṣopāya*, a remarkable, sprawling document telling of the sage Vasiṣṭha's discussions with Rāma and embedding within its text no fewer than sixty-four fabulous philosophical stories, including the story about Rudra I discussed in Chapter 4, and the story about Līlā that I will describe in Chapter 6. These stories are like thought experiments, and they both dramatize the argument Vasiṣṭha wants to make and serve as protreptic, exhortations to Rāma to live a certain kind of life. In one of the most famous stories, the story of Lavaṇa, the protagonist's return is distinguished by a remarkable feature: on his return he goes in search of the people and places among whom, within the simulation, he had lived a long and full life—*and* he finds them again! The story thereby forces us to ask about the relationship between objects within and without a simulation, and for Vasiṣṭha a conclusion follows about the nature of the self.

In the Lavaṇa story there is a background assumption, which we might call the "memory asymmetry." The memory asymmetry is that the protagonist remembers nothing about his or her former life for as long as he or she is within the simulation, but clearly remembers the simulation life when returned outside it. That's not generally true of simulation: it doesn't hold for dreams and it doesn't hold for Hall in *Simulacron-3*. Indeed, it doesn't hold for "In the Forest of Estrangement" either, where, as we have seen, the protagonist in the forest retains memories of his alcove.

I will present the story in an emended version of Wendy Doniger's abridgement:

> In the lush country of the Northern Pāṇḍavas there once reigned a virtuous king named Lavaṇa, born in the family of Hariścandra. One day when Lavaṇa was seated on his throne in the assembly hall, a magician entered, bowed, and said to the king, "While

you sit on your throne, watch this marvellous trick." Then he waved his peacock-feather wand, and a man from Sindh entered, leading a horse; and as the king gazed at the horse, he remained motionless upon his throne, his eyes fixed and staring, as if in meditation. His courtiers were worried, but they remained still and silent, and after a few minutes the king awoke and began to fall from his throne.

Servants caught him as he fell, and the king asked, in confusion, "What is this place? Whose is this hall?" When he finally regained his senses, he told this story: "While I was sitting in front of the horse and looking at the waving wand of the magician, in the confusion of my mind [*ātmanā bhrāntamānasaḥ*; 3.106.5] it seemed that I mounted the horse and went out hunting alone. Carried far away, I arrived at a great desert, which I crossed to reach a jungle, and under a tree a creeper caught me and suspended me by the shoulders. As I was hanging there, the horse went out from under me. I spent the night in that tree, sleepless and terrified. As I wandered about the next day, I saw a dark-skinned young girl carrying a pot of food, and, since I was starving, I asked her for some food. She told me that she was a Caṇḍāla and said that she would feed me only if I married her. I agreed to this, and, after she fed me, she took me back to her village, where I married her and became a foster Caṇḍāla. She bore me two sons and two daughters, and I spent sixty years with her there, wearing a loincloth stinking and mildewed and full of lice, drinking the still-warm blood of wild animals I killed, eating carrion in the cremation grounds. Though I was the only son of a king, I grew old and gray and worn out, and I forgot that I had been a king; I became firmly established as a Caṇḍāla. One day, when a terrible famine arose and an enormous drought and forest fire, I took my family and escaped into another forest. As my wife slept, I said to my younger son, 'Cook my flesh and eat it,' and he agreed to this, as it was his only hope of staying alive. I resolved to die and made a funeral pyre, and, just as I was about

> to throw myself on it, at that very moment, I, the king, fell from this throne. Then I was awakened by shouts of 'Hurrah!' and the sound of music. This is the delusion [*moha*; 3.109.21] that the magician wrought upon me."
>
> As King Lavaṇa finished this speech, the magician suddenly vanished. Then the courtiers, their eyes wide with amazement, said, "My lord, this was no magician; it was divine magic shown to our lord to demonstrate the lot of humanity and the state of the world. Evidently this world is a creation of the mind [3.109.27–8]." The king set out the very next day to go to the desert, having resolved to find once more the wasteland that had been reflected in the mirror of his mind. With his ministers, he wandered until he found an enormous desert just like the one he had known in his thoughts, and to his amazement he discovered all the exact details he had seen [3.120.7]: he recognized outcaste hunters who were his acquaintances, and he found the village where he had been a foster Caṇḍāla, and he saw this and that man, and this and that woman, and all the various things that people use, and the trees that had been withered by the drought, and the orphaned hunter children.
>
> And he saw an old woman who was his mother-in-law. He asked her, "What happened here? Who are you?" She told him the story: a king had come there and married her daughter, and they had had children, and then the drought came and all the villagers died. The king became amazed and full of pity. He asked many more questions, and her answers convinced him that the woman was telling the story of his own experience among the Caṇḍālas. Then he returned to the city and to his own palace, where the people welcomed him back [3.121.8]. (MU 3.104.12–3.121.8; Doniger 1984, 132–134)

We can distinguish the following elements in the story. There is a simulator, the magician, who causes the protagonist, Lavaṇa, to enter a virtual reality environment. Lavaṇa is immersed in this environment, as we infer from the fact that his later report is couched in the first person. Within the simulation, the protagonist has no memory of his life without it, but not vice versa. The simulation is of the protagonist leading a long and full life, although on his return he finds that just a few moments have passed. Exit from the simulation is triggered by a traumatic event within it: he is about to throw himself into a fire. All these elements constitute what I will call the *entrance*, *immersion*, and *exit* phases of the story. The story about Nārada, discussed in Chapter 3, followed the same pattern. There too, the protagonist, Nārada, is thrown into a virtual reality environment, one generated by Viṣṇu, where he undergoes an immersive lived experience, a life as a woman, and then exits it at a moment of crisis. The Lavaṇa story doesn't end there, however, and it is the next phase that lends it its provocative philosophical significance. In this phase—the *comparison* phase of the story, as we might say—Lavaṇa sets off in search of the village and the villagers among whom he had, in the simulation, lived for so long. To his, and our, astonishment, he does indeed discover it. It exists outside the simulation; it was not a *mere* simulation.

The story of Lavaṇa makes two sorts of claim. There is a metaphysical claim and a motivational claim. The metaphysical claim has to do with the identity of objects; what it claims is that virtual objects, the objects within a simulation, are identical to normal objects, objects without the simulation. It is an affirmation of trans-simulation object identity. It needn't be read so strongly as to claim that *every* object within the simulation also exists outside it; it is enough to say that *some* objects within the simulation also exist without. For that already excludes one possibility, which is that the virtual, simulated objects are of a different kind altogether. That is to say, it excludes virtual realism, the view that virtual objects are just as real as other sorts of objects but are made up, for instance, of digital information rather than physical matter (Chalmers 2022). And, importantly, it excludes the notion that simulations are illusions or hallucinations, because the objects in hallucinations and illusions are merely apparent entities; they have no existence or reality outside the hallucination or illusion. For this reason it is quite wrong to translate the Sanskrit term *māyā*, which refers to the magic performed by the magician, as "illusion." Doniger clarifies that "*māyā* is what Rudra makes when he imagines the universe; *māyā* is his art" (1984, 213); it is "a kind of artistic power" (1984, 118), which only later became associated with notions of trickery and deceit (see further Chapter 7).

The motivational claim is that a belief in trans-simulation object identity will lead not to moral panic and existential breakdown but rather to serenity of mind. *Simulacron-3* allows for something like trans-simulation object identity, insofar as Hall himself, at the end of the story, "ascends" to the higher level, as does Ashton, the contact unit within the total simulation environment, if only briefly. Hall is initially racked with feelings of despair and pointlessness, but he eventually finds solace in a belief in the Cartesian *cogito*. Lavaṇa, on the other hand, is meant to find solace in curbing the mind's wanderings (MU 3.121.55).

On hearing this story, Rāma is given to wonder, "How did the dream become true/real [*satya*]? Tell me, good brahmin" (MU 3.121.11; Doniger 1984, 184). Vasiṣṭha says in reply that "the mind experiences precisely the things that it itself causes to arise, though such things are not truly real, nor, on the other hand, are they unreal" (*vāsanāvalitaṃ ceto yad yathā bhāvayaty alam* | | *tat tathānubhavaty āśu na sad asti na cāpy asat*; MU 3.121.16; Doniger 1984, 184).

Realism Retrieved

Two points can be quickly made and set aside. The first point is that we must reject a popular but overly simplistic reading of the story. This "simple reading" would have it that what the story demonstrates, or is intended to demonstrate, is that everything is an illusion, or that idealism is true. The thought goes something like this: the objects within a dream or induced simulation or virtual world are *merely* illusory, and so if they are identical to objects without, then those too are *merely* illusory. Now that would indeed be a terrible argument. For, first, there is no reason to think that virtual or simulated objects are merely illusory: a virtual realist claims that they are real objects made out of data, and Pessoa himself evidently thinks of his heteronyms as more than mere illusions (they do, after all, write poetry). And, second, if we grant the truth of trans-simulation object identity—that is, if we accept at face value the story's assertion that Lavaṇa really can and does rediscover the village—and agree that simulations are illusions, the most that would follow is that the rediscovered village is an illusion. No conclusion could be drawn about the portion of reality that does not mirror anything in his virtual experience (see Chakravarti 2015 for additional arguments against the simple reading). In the Lavaṇa story, it is interesting to note that the courtiers are given to voice this simple interpretation of Lavaṇa's adventure but that this does not coincide with the explanation Vasiṣṭha provides to Rāma. It's a reading of the story that's good enough for commoners but not for kings.

What I am calling the simple reading of Vasiṣṭha's argument in the *Mokṣopāya* is effectively dismissed in certain of Kendall Walton's remarks about the imagination. Walton writes, for example, that

> a conception of imaginative experiences as, in general, free-floating fantasies disconnected from the real world would be narrow and distorted. Sometimes, to be sure, imagining is a means of escape from reality, and we do frequently imagine what is not really the case. But even when we do, our experience is likely to involve the closest attention to features of our actual environment, not a general oblivion to it. Most imaginings are in

> one way or another dependent on or aimed at or anchored in the real world. (Walton 1990, 21)

A conception of the imagination as a power to transcend the world in thought is precisely not what is in play in the *Mokṣopāya*. It is a mystery to Lavaṇa how it comes to be that his magician-induced imaginings are "anchored" in the real world, but anchored they are.

A second but equally deflationary reading of the story would have it that Lavaṇa had the equivalent of a true dream. If dreams can be true, then, as various Buddhist philosophers suggest, they may also provide access to past and future, as well as to the minds of others—that is, premonition and telepathy (Hayashi 2001). Why then would they not also provide access to remote regions to which one has never travelled? Yet the potential truth of a dream, or any other type of simulation, is compatible both with the affirmation of trans-simulation object identity and with its denial. For it could be as with the case of the "true likeness" of a painting, which is to say that a true dream might be a faithful *representation* without involving the very same objects.

Valberg does think that the same objects are experienced both within and without dreams. But he differs from Vaṣiṣtha and Pessoa in that he regards the matter as entirely trivial. He writes:

> In my dream my daughter was seated next to me. So my daughter was in my dream. And by "my daughter" I mean (who else?) my daughter, the girl in school about two miles from this cafe. Let us assume that we know what is going on here, that we are not going to get excited about the fact that, although my daughter and the girl in the dream belong to discrete worlds, I am prepared to say that the girl in the dream was (is) my daughter. . . . Consider [next] the human being (or soul: but we shall ignore for now the possibility that I am a soul) that I am. In the dream, my daughter was sitting next to me. Then I went to get a drink of water. To whom do I refer in this connection by "me" and "I"? Well, to

> whom do I ever refer to by "I"? Why should this case be special? "I" refers to the human being that I am, *this* one (I touch my chest). So it would seem that we can now just transfer what we have said about dreams and identity to the first-person case. If we can handle the superficial puzzlement about my daughter, or this cafe, being in a dream of mine, there should be no special problem about me—the human being that I am, the one who dreamed those past dreams—being in such a dream. The human being I am was part of the world internal to my dream of the other night, and that world is discrete from the world to which *this* human being (I touch him again) belongs. Still, it is correct to say that I, that very human being (the one I touched), was in my dream the other night—just as it is correct to say that my daughter was in that dream. (Valberg 2007, 61–62)

Valberg agrees with Vasiṣṭha in affirming the truth of trans-simulation object identity, that the daughter he dreamt of and the girl who goes to school are one and the same person. He correctly rejects the idea that dreams and other simulations are mere illusions, fabrications whose contents are detached from the world outside the dream. Yet he is quite unlike Vasiṣṭha in that he considers this to be a matter of "superficial puzzlement." I must say that I do not agree with Valberg about this. I side rather with Pessoa, who finds the topic very vexing, writing, "The only problem is that of reality, as insoluble as it is alive. What do I know about the difference between a tree and a dream? I can touch the tree; I know that I have the dream. What is all this really?" (2002, #378). And, again, "Do I, who make you exist in me, have more real life than you?" (2002, 445).

Let us then see whether something else might be going on, the cause of something more than "superficial puzzlement." What is going on, I suggest, is that the story aims to undermine our too-easy habit of thinking about reality in terms of there being different levels or layers or worlds. These metaphors permeate discussions about dreams, simulations, virtual reality, and induced experience of every kind. Metaphors of "ascent" and "descent" between "higher" and "lower" levels run throughout the literature, and it is no coincidence that the term *avatāra* has gained such prominence. The Lavaṇa story, I propose, invites us to escape the grip of these metaphors and to think of the phases of entry and exit instead as movements in a single space, a movement across borders rather than between worlds. Vasiṣṭha says, and I think this is an important clue, that the states of consciousness witnessed respectively in waking and dreaming are just as an actor taking up their parts (*svacittavṛttir eveyaṃ jāgratsvapnadṛśoditā / rasāveśād upādatte śailūṣa iva bhūmikām*; MU 3.110.49). This same analogy appears in other places in our text. The mind, we are informed, goes by different names in different forms (*rūpa*), just as an actor does, and just as the actor gets different names in accordance with the different roles performed, so too does the mind (MU 3.96.43, 3.96.56). The mind is like an actor in moving from one emotion (*bhāva*) to the next, depending on context (3.103.6). Different modes of consciousness are not distinct modes of access to different levels or worlds but rather different performances by the same actor. The same objects turn up in different modes of consciousness, just as a chair used as a prop onstage is still a chair when the performance is over. Vasiṣṭha would have us reject the sort of thinking that puts everything into ontological hierarchies, the sort of levels-think that is exemplified when it is said that the objects described in fundamental physics are at the bottom, foundational level, then above them the objects described in chemistry, biology, the social sciences, and so on. He would have us think instead that there is a single domain of objects, populated by objects versatile enough to figure in different scenes. Viṣṇu speaks of two modes of appearance, one that we take to be mere appearance and one that is taken to be direct access to reality. Precisely that bifurcated way of thinking is what the story seeks to undermine. The universe is indeed plural, but its plurality isn't down to there being different *levels* of reality. Rather, there are different modes of consciousness within which the same objects play different parts.

There seems to be no reason we shouldn't run Vasiṣṭha's argument in terms of episodic memory instead of dreams. Episodic memory involves what Envel Tulving calls autonoetic consciousness, or, more colourfully, "mental time travel." Mental time travel refers to the possibility that a first-person perspective may be located at subjective times other than the personal present. The phrase was introduced by Tulving in the course of explaining a distinction between three modes of consciousness, which he called anoetic, noetic, and autonoetic. A person possesses autonoetic consciousness if she "is capable of becoming aware of her own past as well as her own future; she is capable of mental time travel, roaming at will over what has happened as readily as over what might happen, independently of physical laws that govern the universe" (Tulving 1985, 5). It is manifest in memory when one remembers a past happening as if one were experiencing it again, and in anticipation when one projects oneself into a future experience (for example, by imagining what it will be like). Autonoetic consciousness is thus a capacity to be aware of oneself in one's own personal past or future: it is the name given to "the kind of consciousness that mediates an individual's awareness of his or her existence and identity in subjective time extending from the personal past through the present to the personal future" (Tulving 1985, 1). In its role in episodic memory, Tulving has described it as a capacity to revisit earlier experience, "a unique awareness of re-experiencing here and now something that happened before, at another time and in another place" (Tulving 1993, 68), and also as a capacity for representation, one "that allows adult humans to mentally represent and to become aware of their protracted existence across subjective time" (Wheeler, Stuss, and Tulving 1997, 335) Tulving views autonoesis as the source of a proprietary phenomenology: "It provides the characteristic phenomenal flavour of the experience of remembering. . . . It is autonoetic consciousness that confers the special phenomenal flavour to the remembering of past events, the flavour that distinguishes remembering from other kinds of awareness, such as those characterizing perceiving, thinking, imagining, or dreaming" (Tulving, 2005, 1, 3).

William James put the idea in different words, saying that our reliving and preliving of past and future experience are distinguished by a sort of warmth and intimacy: "A farther condition is required before the present image can be held to stand for a past original. That condition is the fact that the imagined be expressly referred to the past, thought as in the past. . . . But even that would not be memory. Memory requires more than mere dating of a fact in the past. It must be dated in my past. In other words, I must think that I directly experienced its occurrence. It must have . . . 'warmth and intimacy'" (James 1890, 1:650). As the very terminology implies, autonoesis is intended to identify a capacity to know or conceive of oneself in a special way, as having a continuing existence in subjective time, reliving past experiences in their felt pastness and preliving or as-if living future experiences in their felt futurity. When Tulving says that "organisms can behave and learn without [autonoetic] awareness, but they cannot *remember* without awareness" (Tulving 1985, 6), he has in mind the retrieval of past experiences as "personally experienced" (so that "episodic memory mediates the *remembering* of personally experienced events"). In remembering, one is aware of oneself as reexperiencing a past event.

Perhaps I recall an extended episode in my past, and in so doing I relive it "from the inside." It may now feel to me much as the life Lavaṇa led inside his induced experience feels to him. Here too there are two "modes of appearance" for one and the same set of events, which appear to me both as I experienced them in the past and as I now recall them. With such a reformulation in terms of episodic memory, there is no inclination to explain what is going on in terms of a hypothesis about different domains of reality. The point is that if we agree that episodic memory, the *de se* remembering of past events, is a mode of consciousness of events previously perceptually witnessed, then why should we claim anything different about the *de se* imagining of events? There is no reason to accept the premise of the simple reading, which is that imagining as a mode of consciousness accesses a proprietary domain of entities. Pessoa, recall, denies that this is so even of poetry.

All this is as much true of *us* as it is of the objects in our environment. Lavaṇa seemed to himself to be a tribal huntsman, and so it was (*caṇḍālatvaṃ hi lavaṇaḥ pratibhāsavaśād*; 3.110.50–51). Or rather, as we can say now that we have the Pessoan concept of heteronymy to guide us, it is possible for me to enter into new ways of being in the world, involving different modes of attention to it, and to that extent being different selves. Waking and dreaming are but two frames of heteronymy, two theatre stages I might step onto from the wings, and in doing so become different "I"s. Indeed, Vasiṣṭha's argument implies that there is no life offstage: waking is to be thought of not in terms of leading a life out of role but as just one more form of acting. There is no "tribunal of experience": waking life is one life among many, not a source of ultimate verification. There are many ways of having a world in view, and no one way is best or better. This is, I believe, what the *Mokṣopāya* wants to teach us: appealing once more to a theatrical metaphor, the text asserts that mind is an actor whose stage is the world (*jagat*), watched by its troupe (*jagajjālam ayaṃ nṛttam idaṃ cittanaṭais tatam / etayaivaikayā paṅktyā dṛśyate dīpalekhayā*; MU 5.59.29). As there is just one stage, so there is just one world, a single world in which the mind takes up its various parts. Vasiṣṭha's argument is that one is always in role, that wakefulness is just another role alongside other modalities of immersed experience. I think that Pessoa agrees, especially when he talks of "Fernando Pessoa himself" as just one heteronym among the others (the one who is an orthonym, to be exact). All life is, in the end, a life of self-estrangement.

It follows that it would be a mistake to think that ordinary waking perceptual experience is an unmarked category of cognition, somehow more fundamental in our epistemic lives than other modes of consciousness, including memory, testimony, imagination, and simulation. The plurality in the injunction to "be plural like the universe" is epistemic as well as metaphysical. An epistemically plural life is one in which a plurality of "styles of inquiry" into the world or "ways of knowing" the world operate in unison. If a superficial reading of the Lavaṇa story has it support idealism, when we dig deeper into the text we find that what it actually advocates is epistemic pluralism. Just as there are many paths to the summit of a mountain, each with its distinctive strengths and drawbacks, so too are there many ways to get at the world (for a fully developed defence of epistemic pluralism, see Ganeri 2019). Vasiṣṭha is, then, neither a relativist, thinking that the truth is relative to a frame of cognition, nor a scientific naturalist, someone who claims that only one such frame provides guaranteed access to the truth. His view is instead close to what Hubert Dreyfus and Charles Taylor call "pluralistic robust realism." According to this view,

> there may be (1) multiple ways of interrogating reality (that's the "plural" part), which nevertheless (2) reveal truths independent of us, that is truths that require us to revise and adjust our thinking to grasp them (and that's the robust realist part), and where (3) all attempts fail to bring the different ways of interrogating reality into a single mode of questioning that yields a unified picture or theory (so they stay plural). (Dreyfus and Taylor 2015, 154)

Lavaṇa had multiple "ways of interrogating reality," including his everyday perceptual experience, the testimony he receives from the villagers, and his magician-induced simulated experience. They reveal a truth that is independent of him, and yet they cannot be reduced to a single mode of questioning.

I don't deny that we can find in the *Mokṣopāya* formulations of a more idealistic outlook (i.e., the simple reading); indeed, we have seen that outlook put into the mouths of the courtiers in Lavaṇa's palace. Nor do I find plausible the suggestion that all such formulations represent later textual accretions, subsequent "Vedānticizations" of an original ur-text (Slaje 2020). Instead, we can comfortably see the *Mokṣopāya* as another example of a common genre of writing in India, one in which the text is made to reveal progressively more subtle doctrines (*guḍhārtha*) as the reader probes deeper below the surface. The epitome of this genre is, of course, the dialogue between Indra and Prajāpati in the Chāndogya Upaniṣad.

Let me end by returning to Pessoa and to his one and only play. Pessoa wrote *The Mariner* in 1913, at about the same time as he wrote his first published story, "In the Forest of Estrangement," and so just before the heteronyms burst triumphantly onto the scene (in fact, he would later classify both the play and the story as examples of intersectionism [Zenith 2021, 389]). *The Mariner* offers an intriguing parallel with the story of Lavaṇa in the *Mokṣopāya*. The magician's role is played by the second of three watchmen, who one night, to relieve their boredom, describes a dream in which a mariner stranded on an island, to relieve the tedium, dreams of living in a foreign land. The mariner is Lavaṇa, his watchman-induced dream analogous to Lavaṇa's magician-induced experience. Pessoa writes that the mariner

> dreamed up a homeland he'd never had, and he made that other homeland his: another kind of country with other kinds of landscapes, and different people, who had a different way of walking down the street and leaning out their windows. . . . Soon he had a country he'd crossed and recrossed countless times. He remembered having already spent thousands of hours along its coastline. He knew the usual color of twilight on a certain northern bay, and how soothing it was to enter—late at night, with his soul basking in the murmur of the water cut by the ship's prow—a large southern port where he had spent, perhaps happily, his imaginary youth. . . . Soon he had another previous life. . . .

> In this new homeland he already had a birthplace, places where he'd grown up, and ports from where he'd set sail. . . . He began to acquire childhood playmates, and then friends and enemies from his youth. (Pessoa 2001, 27–28)

If this describes the entrance and immersion phases of the simulation, the exit in Pessoa is different. The mariner tries but cannot remember his former life outside the dream (the "memory asymmetry" assumption is in play here too), and "one day a boat arrived . . . One day a boat arrived. . . . Yes, yes . . . that has to be what happened. . . . One day a boat arrived, and passed by that island, and the mariner wasn't there" (2001, 29). For Pessoa, it is not the mariner but the watchman for whom a bafflement arises: he is given to wonder, in another resonance with Zhuangzi's butterfly, "Why can't the mariner be the only thing in all of this that's real, and we and everything else just one of his dreams?" And then he is made to wonder, "Wouldn't we be better off shutting ourselves up in our dream and forgetting life, so that death would in turn forget us?" The second watchman's anxiety is that of Doug Hall or Ashton in *Simulacron-3*, an existential worry about one's status if the simulation hypothesis is true.

The most intriguing novelty in Pessoa's story, though, is the idea of the mariner being swallowed up by his own dream. For surely to say this is to reject, once again, the idea that the world outside the dream and the world within constitute two autonomous metaphysical domains. As his life within the dream gains substance, his life outside it fades away, and if a dream can reach out and incorporate the dreamer into itself, then that can be only because there is no hard metaphysical border between what is within the dream and what is without. And Pessoa only restates Vasiṣṭha's thesis when he says elsewhere, "Things are the raw material of my dreams; that's why I apply a distractedly hyper-attentive attention to certain details of the Outside. . . . In dreams we do not, as in reality, focus equally on the important and unimportant aspects of an object. . . . I haven't really fled from life, in the sense of seeking a softer bed for my soul; I've merely changed lives, finding in my dreams the same objectivity that I found in life" (2002, 433–434). Pessoa, evidently, is no idealist: dreams are not illusions, and the existence of the same objects both inside and outside dreams does not entail that the objects encountered in daily life are illusions either.

My suggestion has been that the creation of heteronyms itself represents a form of epistemic pluralism, now about self-knowledge. Each heteronym is a distinct "way of interrogating" the self, and it is perhaps only by allowing oneself to inhabit a plurality of heteronymic first-personal stances that one can achieve knowledge of one's self in all its facets. This is how the metaphysical claim and the motivational claim are related to each other: if what motivates one is a search for knowledge of the self (and such has been a cardinal motivation for engaging in philosophy from the time of Socrates and the Upaniṣads), then a heteronymic account of the plurality of selfhood is what is required.

6
Names Used Twice Over

Second Līlā

Fernando Pessoa's relationship with his heteronyms is complicated. They exist as protagonists in imaginary stories of his own creation, and Pessoa imagines himself as them, or imagines being them: "But since I am me, I merely take a little pleasure in the little that it is to imagine myself as that someone else. Yes, soon he-I, under a tree or bower, will eat twice what I can eat, drink twice what I dare drink, and laugh twice what I can conceive of laughing. Soon he, now I. Yes, for a moment I was someone else: in someone else I saw and lived this human and humble joy of existing as an animal in shirtsleeves" (2002, #374). In "Notes for the Memory of My Master Caeiro," Pessoa has Caeiro suggest that things thus seen in "dreams"—that is to say, in acts of imagination—have much the same status as things seen in pictures:

> Fernando Pessoa turned to Caeiro. "Tell me this," he said, pointing his cigarette: "How do you regard dreams? Are they real or not?" "I regard dreams as I regard shadows," answered Caeiro unexpectedly with his usual divine quickness. "A shadow is real, but it's less real than a stone. A dream is real—otherwise it wouldn't be a dream—but it's less real than a thing." . . . "And what do you call a stone that you see in a dream?" asked Fernando, smiling. "I call it a dream," answered my master Caeiro. "I call it a dream of a stone." . . . "Why do you say 'of a stone'? Why do you employ the word 'stone'?" "For the same reason that you, when you see my picture, say 'That's Caeiro' and don't mean that it's me

Fernando Pessoa. Jonardon Ganeri, Oxford University Press. © Oxford University Press 2024.
DOI: 10.1093/oso/9780197636688.003.0007

> in the flesh." We all broke out laughing. "I see and I give up," said Fernando, laughing with the rest of us. (2001, 43–46)

Fernando asks an excellent question here, and Caeiro gives an equally excellent reply. For we do use the name of the picture's subject matter in order to refer to its depiction: we say, pointing to a portrait hanging on the wall, "That is Devadatta."

The use of a name twice over seems to be a characteristic hallmark of heteronymy. We have already encountered the five Indras and the one hundred Rudras. And there is another story in the *Mokṣopāya*, one that is just as famous as the previous two: the story of the two Līlās.

> Queen Līlā was the wife of King Padma. When he died, Līlā prayed to the goddess Sarasvatī, who explained to her that in a former birth Padma and Līlā had been a sage named Vasiṣṭha and his wife Arundhatī; she also told Līlā that the king had now been reborn as King Vidūratha. Since Līlā had not been reborn, the king had taken a new wife, whose name just happened to be Līlā. Sarasvatī used her magic powers to transport herself and Queen Līlā through the air to the palace where King Vidūratha lived; invisible, they saw him in his court. When a great battle took place, they went to the battlefield; there Līlā caught sight of the second Līlā, who had the very same form as hers, like a reflection in a mirror. Puzzled at this, the first Līlā asked Sarasvatī how there could be another woman just like her. The Goddess replied with a long lecture on the projection of mental images from inside to outside, as in dreams. These words were overheard by the second Līlā, who spoke to Sarasvatī and said, "In my dreams I have often spoken with a goddess of wisdom, and she looked exactly as you look to me right now." . . . The first Līlā said [to Vidūratha], "I am Līlā, your queen from a former life. This second Līlā is your queen by my art [*helayā mayā*], produced for you by me; she is just a reflection." (MU 3.15.19ff.; Doniger 1984, 101–102)

Sarasvatī, as Daniel Galouye might have put it, has Līlā "cut in" to the virtual reality in which Vidūratha lives as the heteronym of her deceased husband Padma. She is cut in on a personal surveillance circuit and so, had she been visible, it would have appeared, as Ashton put it, as if "a god dropped down and started talking to you." What does she see? That she is already there on an empathy circuit, that her heteronym is present and even has her name. She declares herself to have made this "second Līlā," who is, she says, her own reflection. In one of those metaphysical backflips for which the *Mokṣopāya* is so well loved, this second Līlā says that she has seen a second Sarasvatī in her dreams, thereby insinuating that her—second Līlā's—claim on reality is no less shaky than that of Līlā the first. If one were to try to construct a Pessoan version of this story, it would be one in which the author of "Notes for the Memory of My Master Caeiro" drops himself in on the get-together in order to witness the second Fernando Pessoa holding forth there. In fact, orthonymy is just a special case of the use of a name twice over. Līlā's reflection is called "Līlā" (specifically, "second Līlā"), just as Caeiro depicted is also called "Caeiro" and Caeiro imagined or dreamt is still called "Caeiro."

We have encountered this same semantic phenomenon before. For Valberg too uses a name twice over in setting up his example of the positional conception of self. Valberg writes, "In my dream I was not JV." The name "Valberg" has been used twice here, first to refer to the dreaming subject, and second to refer to an object within the dream. The point he wants to make with his example is that this object, "JV," is not the immersed subject *within* the dream, the subject picked out by a positional use of the first person. Our problem now, however, is to understand how the same name is used twice. A virtual realist such as Chalmers will make sense of the double use in the following way. They will say that what is seen within a simulation are virtual objects. There is a virtual object, JV, and there is an object outside the simulation, Valberg, and these are different objects, because one is made of digital information and the other of carbon molecules. The different objects are, however, closely related insofar as one is a simulacrum of the other, and that is how we use the same name twice. The semantic rule is something like "The name N of *x* can be used to refer to a simulacrum of *x*." The virtual realist Lambert Wiesing describes virtual objects as "artificial presences" and says, "A virtual reality is only given if the image no longer serves as a medium for referring to something absent, but rather if the image becomes a medium by which a particular kind of object is produced and presented—an object, that is, that is exclusively visible and yet, like a ghost, acts as if it had a substance and the properties of a substance" (Wiesing 2010, 100). The same is true, according to Bence Nanay, of pictures. In a picture, he claims, there is an "encoded object," which is not identical to the subject matter of the picture (Nanay 2018).

For all these thinkers there is an entity, be it a virtual object, an artificial presence, or an encoded object, which serves as a simulacrum of *x* and to which the name N of *x* can therefore be applied. Just why do we use names twice over when we say, pointing at a painting, "This is Devadatta," instead of saying "This is a painting of Devadatta"? We do the same in theatre too, saying "Here is Śakuntalā" even as an actor playing Śakuntalā enters from the wings. In neither case is it plausible to say that we are suffering under an illusion, that we *misperceive* the painting as its subject matter, or the actor as the character. We know full well that it is a painting, and we are as happy to comment on the painting's style, brushwork, provenance, and so on as on the actor's performance. It has become customary to say, instead, that we see Devadatta in the painting, and *seeing-in* requires that we attend both to what is depicted and to the depicting material itself (Wollheim 1980, 142). The virtual realist says that we use the same name twice over because the virtual object, whether in an immersive simulation or in a two-dimensional picture, is a stand-in for or simulacrum of an actual object.

This is, I suggest, the kind of view Vasiṣṭha wants Rāma to reject. There is just one Līlā, inside and outside the simulation, where here the simulation is a Sarasvatī-generated glimpse of the afterlife, just as there is only one village in the Lavaṇa story. "Līlā" and "second Līlā" are two uses of a name to refer to the same person, Līlā. This is partly to agree with Valberg when he writes (as noted in Chapter 5) that "the human being I am was part of the world internal to my dream of the other night, and that world is discrete from the world to which *this* human being (I touch him again) belongs. Still, it is correct to say that I, that very human being (the one I touched), was in my dream the other night—just as it is correct to say that my daughter was in that dream" (Valberg 2007, 62). Valberg, however, muddies the waters by importing talk of different "worlds," and for that reason his view is confused. A world can be only, if anything, a proprietary domain of objects. This imports a commitment to a layered conception of reality: fundamental physics has elementary particles, mechanics has ordinary middle-sized objects, biology has plants and animals, the social sciences have social groups and communities, and so on. Hardly a matter of "superficial puzzlement," it is instead an outright impossibility that the very same object could show up in two discrete worlds. In a similar vein, the *Mokṣopāya* is typically depicted as a work "teaching a variety of esoteric knowledge meant to liberate an aspirant from the vagaries of the phenomenal world" (Nair 2020, 1). Pessoa is clearer, and is clearly on Vasiṣṭha's side: "This new reality—that of a strange forest—makes its appearance without effacing the reality of my warm alcove. . . . And that tremulous, transparent landscape clearly belongs to them both" (2002, 417). The presence of objects in both of two fields of experience is what Pessoa calls "intersectionism" (see Ganeri 2021, 33–40).

A tempting alternative is to associate each of the two uses of a name with a distinct route to its single referent. When Gottlob Frege introduced the concept of a "mode of presentation" into the philosophy of language, his aim was to explain how it could be that the identity between Hesperus and Phosphorus, the morning star and the evening star, both of which are none other than the planet Venus, can be informative (Frege 1980). If both names refer to the same object, why isn't it true a priori that one is identical to the other? It isn't true a priori, Frege pointed out, because the same object is given twice over, under two different modes of presentation. Yet Frege will help us only so far in solving the mystery of the two Līlās. For consider again Lavaṇa. He was certainly surprised to discover the village, the very same village he had gotten to know so well while under the magician's spell. But his surprise wasn't the result of discovering that the village he was now seeing and the village he had gotten to know so well were, after all, one and the same. He knew that from the first moment he came across it; indeed, he went in search of it. He didn't think that here is a village and there was a village, and only then discover that they were one and the same village. That wasn't the source of his surprise. What surprised him was that the village should be there at all: how is it possible that my village, the village in which I lived for so many years, should be *here*? It's the same for Līlā. When Sarasvatī gives her a peek into the afterlife, she is certainly surprised to find Līlā there, but her sense of surprise isn't due to the discovery that this Līlā is her after all. Her surprise is of the form: what am I doing *here*? Like Lavaṇa, she is presented as extremely vexed that the same things that appeared in her glimpse of the afterlife are also in the here and now, and she marvels at Sarasvatī's artistic power (*māyā*), which is such that "the same high hills, the same spacious forests of palm and *hintāla* trees are both on the outside as well as inside myself" (MU 3.18.4). She tries to rationalize it to herself by likening her new and alarming situation to the workings of a mirror, the very same objects that are outside being reflected in it. And that does seem right: if I see the sun reflected in a windowpane, I might sometimes be mistaken about the sun's location, but it is certainly the sun I am seeing. Līlā nevertheless resolves to ask Sarasvatī which is truly real (*pāramārthika*) and which erroneous (*bhrānti*) (MU 3.18.5–6).

Nor is the surprise Lavaṇa and Līlā experience akin to the one John Perry experienced when he tracked a trail of sugar on a supermarket floor, pushing his shopping trolley up and down the aisles in a hunt for the shopper with a torn bag of sugar, only for him finally to realize that he himself was the shopper he was trying to chase down (1979, 3). Certainly it can be starting to discover that a person presented under some description is, after all, oneself, but that wasn't what startled Lavaṇa or Līlā, or indeed the other protagonists of the stories in the *Mokṣopāya*. Their question wasn't "Is this the same village?" or "Are these the same trees?" or "Is this me?" Their question was "How can this village be *here*?" and "How can I be *here*?" They are already, as it is sometimes said, immune to any error due to misidentification.

Imagining Seeing Yourself

What is it, then, that causes Lavaṇa and Līlā to be surprised? It is precisely the discovery that there is only one world, not two. Lavaṇa had thought, on emerging from the magician's spell, that he had been taken to a world of illusion, a world whose contents don't really exist. The lesson he is taught is that this was never the case. He was taken not to another world but to the same world differently made present. He hadn't known that *how* the world is made present matters just as much as *what* is made present. He had taken it for granted that there is just one correct way to have the world in view, just one correct way of interrogating reality. What surprises him is the discovery that this is not the case, that there is more than one correct way to have the world in view. Lavaṇa led two lives, one under the magician's spell and another free of it—indeed, three, if one agrees that there is a discontinuity between his life before and his life afterwards—and the experiential quality of each of those lives, as manifested, for example, in the sense of time passing, is linked with their different ways of apprehending the world.

Matters are exactly the same, and perhaps more explicitly so, with Pessoa. Pessoa-as-Caeiro leads one sort of life, while Pessoa-as-Campos leads another. It isn't surprising or informative that there is one Pessoa here; what really is surprising is the discovery that it is possible to live a plurality of lives. In a way, this is the quintessence of Pessoa's philosophy, that it makes explicit something easily overlooked in what it is to lead a life.

Recouching the matter in terms of imagination rather than celestial intervention we might say that Līlā (= first Līlā) imagined herself (= second Līlā) at the side of her husband in the afterlife. The oddness of the story comes from something else she imagines. She imagines *seeing* herself beside her husband in the afterlife. That is to say, she (Līlā, the imagining subject) imagines herself (Līlā, the immersed subject) seeing herself (Līlā, an object in the imagined scene) beside her husband in the afterlife. When Līlā imagines seeing herself it is as if she is present twice over, and that is the reason for all the talk of first and second Līlā. Līlā thinks, "In Sarasvatī's simulation, I am Līlā seeing myself, Līlā, standing beside my husband." Here we have the same name used twice without there being two Līlās. It has been used the first time to refer to Līlā imagined "from the inside," the one at the centre of a perspective on the scene, a scene presented Līlāesquely. And it has been used the second time to refer to Līlā imagined "from the outside," seen standing beside Vidūratha. Līlā's surprise, then, is a surprise at encountering herself located somewhere other than at the perspectival centre.

The Līlā story is in fact a good illustration of what François Recanati has called "explicit *de se* imagining" (2007, 199), as contrasted with the "implicit *de se* imagining" we discussed when thinking about what it might mean to imagine being someone else. Recanati writes that "we may imagine something about ourselves by adopting an external point of view—the point of view of an outside observer" (2007, 199). Zeno Vendler's example of the phenomenon in question is the most famous. Vendler writes:

> We are looking down upon the ocean from a cliff. The water is rough and cold, yet there are some swimmers riding the waves. "Just imagine swimming in that water," says my friend, and I know what to do. "Brr!" I say as I imagine the cold, the salty taste, the tug of the current, and so forth. Had he said "Just imagine *yourself* swimming in that water," I could comply in another way too: by picturing myself being tossed about, a scrawny body bobbing up and down in the foamy waste. In this case, I do not have to leave the cliff in the imagination: I may see myself, if I so choose, from the very same perspective. Not so in the previous case: if I indeed imagine being in the water, then I may see the cliff above me, but not myself from it. (1979, 161)

Recanati notes that this is a case in which the subject imagines *seeing* himself swim in the water, and comments, "The subject plays two roles: he is not only the experiencer, the person from whose point of view the scene is seen, but he is also an object in the scene. This duality enables the subject to look at himself (herself) from an external, third person point of view" (2007, 196). In an exactly analogous manner, Līlā imagines *seeing* herself standing beside Vidūratha. She too plays a double role, both as the immersed subject, located at the centre of the point of view from which the scene is seen ("first Līlā"), and as an object in that scene ("second Līlā"). Recanati observes that there is no question of the subject's rightly or wrongly identifying himself or herself as the person his or her imagination is about, because "what one's imagination is about is a matter of intentional stipulation and does not have to be identified" (2007, 199). There is, in other words, no possibility of error due to misidentification. Rather, what makes it a case of explicit *de se* is that two conditions are satisfied: first, that "the subject must think of the object of his/her imagination as himself/herself," and second, that "the subject must represent himself/herself from an objective point of view, that is, from outside" (2007, 199). The fact that our case satisfies these two conditions explains why it is both uninformative and yet surprising—uninformative because it is imagining *de se*, but surprising because second Līlā is represented (to herself) from outside. Surely the possibility of this sort of double role is the reason the double in literature is such a powerful and popular trope. It is also the mechanism involved in all Pessoa's orthonymic writings.

A Common Ground?

If it is possible to imagine seeing the world in different ways, then it seems to follow that one's way of seeing the world is a continent feature of oneself. This realization might lead one to wonder if it would be possible to do away with every way of seeing the world altogether. Vasiṣṭha's not unreasonable suggestion is that one then hits a bedrock of consciousness that underwrites any way of seeing. He calls it "cosmic consciousness" (*cid-ākāśa*). The very lengthy sixth book of the *Mokṣopāya*, the *Nirvāṇa Prakaraṇa*, is an extended eulogy to this state of mind. I will postpone until Chapter 8 a survey of the enduring influence of this concept of "universal" or "cosmic" consciousness. Some of Pessoa's remarks do make it seem as if he again sides with Vasiṣṭha here. He talks of being a "medium" and a "meeting place" for the heteronyms: "Today I have no personality: I've divided all my humaneness among the various authors whom I've served as literary executor. Today I'm the meeting-place of a small humanity that belongs only to me. . . . I subsist as a kind of medium of myself, but I'm less real than the others, less substantial, less personal, and easily influenced by them all" (2001, 262). He says, "I created a nonexistent coterie, placing it all in a framework of reality. I ascertained the influences at work and the friendships between them, I listened in myself to their discussions and divergent points of view, and in all of this it seems that I, who created them all, was the one who least there" (2001, 257). To think of oneself as a "meeting-place" with no personality of its own is to think that there is a sort of self-awareness more primitive than that of having an individuated point of view (in Ganeri 2021, I call this "forumnal" self-awareness). Zeno Vendler approaches the same idea when he asks, "What are these 'I's that we can shed and don at will as so many costumes, and what is this 'I' that performs the change?" (1984, 26), answering that, as regards the "I" that performs the change, "here the I does not pick out an object, a thing, in the field of consciousness; it marks the ultimate subject, the transcendental self" (1984, 106).

Are we not, though, in danger once again of committing what I called in Chapter 1 the "chameleon without any colour" fallacy? From the fact that a chameleon only contingently has any particular colour, it doesn't follow that it is possible for the chameleon to have no colour at all. Such talk reveals how easy it is to slide from "without any identity in particular" to "without any identity at all." We may prefer a less inflationary interpretation of Pessoa's remarks about meeting places and mediums. That is, we may take such talk to refer to Pessoa the human being rather than to an invariant "I." It is worth noting that when the theatrical metaphor crops up in the *Mokṣopāya* it is sometimes deployed in exactly this deflationary way. We are told, for example, that the mind is an actor on the stage that is its body (MU 3.110.19), and, as noted before, that the mind is the actor whose stage is the world (*jagat*), watched by its troupe (MU 5.59.29). If Pessoa's heteronyms are actors-in-role, the stage upon which they perform is, likewise, the body. We will then interpret forumnal self-awareness to be a proprioceptive awareness of one's own body, something that presumably remains fixed even as heteronymic self-awareness shifts. When Pessoa writes that he is a fugitive, I suggest we read this as meaning that he is always on the run from one identity to another, not that he is running away from any identity at all:

I'm a fugitive.
I was shut up in myself
As soon as I was born.
But I managed to flee.

If people get tired
Of being in the same place,
Why shouldn't they tire
Of having the same self?

My soul seeks me out,
But I keep on the run
And sincerely hope
I'll never be found.

Oneness is a prison.
To be myself is to not be.
I'll live as a fugitive
But live really and truly. (Pessoa 2006, 315)

In a poem he calls "Autopsychography" Pessoa writes,

The poet is a faker
Who's so good at his act
He even fakes the pain
Of pain he feels in fact. (Pessoa 1998, 247)

There is just one pain, a pain both "felt in fact" and "faked." What poets do is dramatize emotions (as so well described in the *rasa* theory of classical Sanskrit aesthetics), and that is not to fictionalize them. Just as there is one village, a village Lavaṇa sees both "in fact" and under the magician's spell, and there is one forested hillside, which Līlā sees both "in fact" and when peeking into the afterlife, there is one Līlā, embodied "in fact" and in imagination. If there is fakery here, it lies with the false idea that there is only one correct way of feeling the pain. What truly astonishes us is to discover that the pain one imagines feeling is *just as real* as the pain one feels "in fact," and, more generally, that there are as many ways to feel, to attend, to experience as there are ways to be alive.

***

And this, in the end, brings us full circle, to the poet of attention and his oath to be plural. With this my own philosophical experiments in intertwining the ideas of Pessoa with those of classical India also reach their end. This has been an exercise in what I call "cosmopolitan philosophy," a philosophy without borders. In the two remaining chapters of this book, I will delve into Pessoa's intellectual engagement with India, these two last chapters belonging therefore to intellectual history rather than philosophy. For, due in large measure to his fascination with neopaganism, Pessoa was unusually interested in, and receptive towards, ideas from India, albeit in the Orientalized form in which they came to him.

PART IV

PESSOA'S IMAGINARY INDIA

7
Pessoa in India

Imagining India

India occupies a curious place in Fernando Pessoa's imagination. Though declaring in a letter to Ofélia Queiroz that it is a country he had wanted to visit (Pessoa 2007, 141), India seems rather to have functioned as a symbol of the exotic and faraway, a destination to travel to in one's imagination rather than in actuality, an emblem of the outer reaches of inner vision: "Nothing is worse than the contrast between the natural splendour of the inner life, with its natural Indias and its unexplored lands, and the squalor of life's daily routine," he says (2002, #445). We will, he promises, "depart in search of a new India, that does not exist in space, in carracks that are built 'of what dreams are made of'" (AP 3101). India is again a "spiritual" destination when he adds, continuing the metaphor, that "this is the first carrack that departs for the Spiritual Indies seeking the Maritime Path through the mists of the soul, that the detours, errors, and backwardness of the present civilization have raised!" (AP 1218).

An imaginary India makes an appearance, too, in Pessoa's reflections on the internal logic of imperialism. In a series of taxonomic remarks, Pessoa identifies three varieties of imperialism: imperialisms of domination, expansion, and culture—that is to say, of power, territory, and spirit (AP 1007). Imperialisms of domination follow the Prussian, Roman, or Austrian model, their respective ambitions being unification, aggrandisement, and hegemony. Imperialisms of expansion believe themselves to be colonizing lands that, if occupied at all, are populated only by the

Fernando Pessoa. Jonardon Ganeri, Oxford University Press. © Oxford University Press 2024.
DOI: 10.1093/oso/9780197636688.003.0008

uncivilized; or lands occupied by people whose civilization, once great, is now degenerate; or, finally, the lands of people who are indeed civilized but too weak to resist. The imperialist views the colonization of the lands of the uncivilized as justified on the grounds that such lands are, by virtue of their climate and geography, incapable of indigenously producing civilization (AP 1013). Brazil is cited as a recipient of this sort of imperialism, while Germany's occupation of Belgium is offered as a case of imperial expansion of the last sort, the justification here appealing simply to the law that might makes right.

India, now imagined as a land whose people, though once civilized, have lapsed into degeneracy, is placed into the second category. Imperial rule of this sort is only ever for the benefit of the colonizer, never the colonized, and the logical consequence of the self-serving justification is that even the enslavement of Indians is permissible:

> Secondly, there is the occupation of territories inhabited by peoples not yet savage or uncivilizable but degenerated from a most ancient civilization. It is the case of India—perhaps even the case of Mexico, just as the Spaniards found it. Here, there is no longer the same simplicity in the right that the expansionist people had to occupy these territories. Let us always recall that the end of colonization and occupation of territories is not civilizing the people that are there, but rather to take to those territories elements of civilization. The end is not altruistic but purely egotistical and civilizational. It is the prolongation of its own civilization that expansive imperialism searches and must search; it is not in any way the advantages that can arise for the inhabitants of that country. Slavery is logical and legitimate; a Zulu or a landim [indigenous Mozambican soldier in the colonial-era Portuguese army] does not represent anything useful in this world. To civilize him, either religiously or in any other way, is to want to give to him that thing that he cannot have. The legitimate [thing] is to oblige him,

> seeing as he is not a person serving the ends of civilization. To enslave him is what is logical; the degenerate egalitarian concept with which Christianity poisoned our social concepts, however, harmed this logical attitude. People like the English hypocritized the concept, and thus managed to serve civilization. (AP 1013)

Though the egalitarianism implicit in Christianity is a threat to imperial expansion, the British were able, hypocritically, to understand its commandments in a manner such that their imperial ambitions were not thwarted. If the governed people deserve, by their degeneracy, to be colonized, then their enslavement is a justifiable way to make them contribute to civilization. With reference to their respective colonies in India, Pessoa draws a contrast between the British and the Portuguese:

> Indians from English India say that they are Indian, those from Portuguese India that they are Portuguese. This, which does not come from any calculation of ours, is the key to our possible future domain. Because the essence of great imperialism is to convert others into our substance, the conversion of others into ourselves. (AP 3438)

The "conversion of others into ourselves" is, indeed, the hallmark of a third variety of imperialism, the cultural imperialism that "does not seek to dominate materially, but influence, dominate through psychic absorption. (It is an imperialism of spiritual expansion.— France is the great example.)" (AP 1007).

The colonization of colonial subjects' subjectivity, an imperialism of spiritual rather than material expansion, is the ultimate imperialist ideal. Interestingly, Indian intellectuals who opposed the British colonial occupation disagreed with Pessoa's claim that Britain had achieved only an imperialism of territorial appropriation. The philosopher Krishnachandra Bhattacharyya (1875–1949), for example, whose brilliant ideas about selfhood and subjectivity Pessoa would have deeply admired, issued a plea for freedom from what he called "cultural subjection," a deeply insidious and almost invisible intellectual slavery. The plea was contained in a talk delivered in Candranagar in October 1931 but not published in his lifetime; Bhattacharyya called this freedom "svarāj in ideas," an intellectual freedom, as contrasted with the "Hind svarāj" or political freedom championed by Mahatma Gandhi (Bhattacharyya [1931] 1954). Bhattacharyya says that "cultural subjection is ordinarily of an unconscious character and it implies slavery from the very start. . . . There is cultural subjection only when one's traditional cast of ideas and sentiments is superseded without comparison or competition by a new cast representing an alien culture which possesses one like a ghost." The sources of subjection lie not so much in the mere fact that the new culture is alien as that it has been allowed to supersede unconsciously and "without comparison or competition," for Bhattacharyya is precise that "assimilation need not be an evil; it may be positively necessary for healthy progress and in any case it does not mean a lapse of freedom." Assimilation, for him, is not a mere "patchwork of ideas of different cultures" nor a "hybridization of ideas," but consists in that kind of synthesis or adjustment or adaptation in which "the foreign ideal is to be assimilated to our ideal and not the other way round," for "it is wrong not to accept an ideal that is felt to be a simpler and deeper expression of our own ideas simply because it hails from a foreign country. . . . The guru or teacher has to be accepted when he is found to be a real guru, whatever the community from which he comes." Assimilation is governed by a principle according to which the assimilated idea, even if alien in origin, is a simpler or deeper expression of an idea that is already one's own; foreign ideas need to be treated with "critical reserve and not docile acceptance . . . docile acceptance without criticism would mean slavery." For Bhattacharyya, then, the British have indeed been successful in a campaign of spiritual imperialism, and this mental subjection needs to be resisted through a moderate and rational retrieval of India's intellectual past (for further discussion, see Ganeri 2017).

In short, when Pessoa assumes the voice of an apologist for imperialism, the "India" that is imagined is the one that must exist if the justification of colonial rule is to be convincing. Pessoa rather elegantly shows how a classic Orientalist trope, that of India as a great ancient civilization that fell into ruin, is key to imperialism's ability to believe itself to be in the right. When, on the other hand, he assumes the heteronymic voice of Bernardo Soares, it is within the metaphor of the soul undertaking its own inner journeys that "India" figures as imaginary destination: "To dream is to find ourselves. You're going to be the Columbus of your soul. You're going to set out to discover your own landscapes" (2002, 400).

An "Indian Ideal"

The philosophical idea Pessoa seems most strongly to associate with India is the idea that the entire world is an illusion. He attributes the idea to Buddhism and Hinduism, more or less indiscriminately, and he is vexed as much by its ethical and aesthetic implications as by its metaphysical status. It is under the heteronym António Mora that many of his discussions of this idea take place. The religions of India are "hyperdeliriums" (AP 1533), in the following sense:

> Buddhism and, before it, the religion of India represent the purest type of distance from the naturally human principles that the collector of disease may wish to find. Departing, clearly or obscurely, from the inhuman principle that life is an illusion, the Buddhist or the brahmanist (??) aims, in his religious cult [worship], to transcend this miserable humanity. (AP 3886)

The metaphysical principle—and Pessoa, qua Mora, isn't sure if it is Buddhist or Brahmanical or both—that life is an illusion seems to him to have as its inevitable ethical corollary that leading a human life is something not to be enjoyed but rather to be "transcended." Elsewhere, Pessoa puts his point in a perfectionist vocabulary: the imperfection of a human life consists in its being mere appearance, and this is what has to be transcended. This is what he calls the "Indian ideal":

> By the last of the same criteria [we] will have life as imperfect by judging it consubstantiated with imperfection, that is, nonexistent, because nonexistence, being the supreme negation, is the absolute imperfection. [We] will have an illusory life not yet imperfect, like for the Greeks, by not being perfect, not yet imperfect, like for the Christian, by being vile and material; otherwise imperfect by not existing, by being mere appearance, absolute appearance, therefore vile, if vile, not so much with vileness of what is vile as with the vileness of what is false. It is from this concept of imperfection that that form of the ideal that is familiarly known to us in Buddhism is born, even though its manifestations arose in India long before that mystical system, both children, him and her, of the same metaphysical substrate. It is true that this ideal appears in diverse forms and applications, with symbolic spiritualists, or occultists, of almost all denominations. As, however, it was in India that the formal manifestations of it distinctively appeared, [we] could be imprecise, however [we] will not be inexact, if we grant to this ideal, by convenience, the name of "Indian ideal." (AP 3123)

Pessoa seems to be channelling Nietzsche in regarding the implied morality of the "Indian ideal" as one of "naysaying" when he says that what distinguishes Indian polytheism from Greek paganism is its "life-denying" quality:

> In Indian religion, on the contrary, the qualities that elevate man to superman are qualities whereby one denies life; [they]

> are ascetic qualities, charitable practices that vitiate individual and civic egoism, the sum of renunciations that contradicts the normal pleasure that normal man has in life. Luckily, the similarity between these two systems is purely external. (AP 3909)

In ethics, asceticism and renunciation are the qualities of the "Indian ideal" associated with human perfection. In aesthetics, to someone who thinks in this way ornamental works of art appear merely as "flowers born withered on the stem of a lie" (AP 3123), beauty residing only in what transcends our humanity. In another remark assigned to the heteronym António Mora, Pessoa summarizes the point:

> From here, [we] see what will be, and in fact is, the difference between the substance of Christian aesthetics and the Hindu (oriental) aesthetics. For the Christian, beauty is in everything that clearly makes us feel our own personality; for the oriental, in everything that transcends our personality. (Pessoa 1996, 243)

The "Indian ideal" is thus one of transcendence, the transcendence of the illusion that is living a human life. Again as Mora, Pessoa writes "*transcendentalism*: Hindu system" (Pessoa quoted in Teixeira 2002).

From where might Pessoa have derived his seemingly firm conviction that there is a pan-Indian "Indian ideal," one that consists in a belief that the world and all human life is an illusion, and which has as an ethics and aesthetics of transcendence as its logical outcome? Perhaps from George Mead, who, in his book *Quests Old and New*, writes that "the dominant philosophical thought of India is based, as is well known, on the conviction that there is but one absolute reality and all else is fiction (*māyā*)" (Mead 1913, 248; see also Cardiello and Gori 2016). Pessoa's own copy of Mead's book is richly annotated, as is his copy of Victor Henry's *Les Littératures de l'Inde: sanscrit, pâli, prâcrit*, in which we can read: "Pour le

Vedānta, l'âme individuelle n'est, encore une fois, qu'une illusion entre toute celles qu'éparpille autour de soi Brahmā le seul vivant [For the Vedānta, the individual soul is, once again, only one of the illusions that Brahmā [*sic*], the only living [conscious?] being, scatters around him]" (Henry 1904, 75). Pessoa has underlined this sentence. Another book owned by Pessoa is Jules de Gaultier's *De Kant à Nietzsche* (Gaultier 1910), in which Gaultier affirms a deep affinity between the philosophies of Hinduism and Kant. Mattia Riccardi observes that Gaultier's "fanciful link between Kantianism and Hinduism is based on the idea that both endorse the view that the 'real' world is nothing but an 'illusion'" (Riccardi 2012, 36).

Pessoa's "Indian ideal" appears, then, to be something of a commonplace within early twentieth-century European Indology. Its textual source will have been the popular and simplified understanding of the Advaita metaphysics of one particular Indian philosopher, the eighth-century Vedāntin Śaṅkara. Śaṅkara indeed read into the Upaniṣads a monist and idealist metaphysics. Drawing on such Upaniṣadic statements as "One should recognize the illusion [*māyā*] as primal matter, and the illusionist [*māyin*] as the great Lord. This whole living world is thus pervaded by things that are parts of him" (Śvetāśvatara Upaniṣad 4.1.10; Olivelle 1998, 425), Śaṅkara suggests that it is only within a cosmic illusion produced by the one absolute real being, *brahman*, that things in the world, including individual human lives, appear as distinct from one another. Another source will have been the *Mokṣopaya* or *Yogavāsiṣṭha*. As I pointed out in Chapters 5 and 6, this text admits of what I called a "simple reading," a reading not so different from the idea Pessoa refers to as the "Indian ideal." This reading entered the popular imagination, even if, as I have argued at length, there is a very different—realist as opposed to idealist—level of meaning in the text. European Indologists habitually, but incorrectly, translated the word *māyā* as "illusion" instead of "artistic power" (Doniger 1984, 118).

I should be clear that in the long history of the Sanskrit intellectual cosmopolis, which ran from the first century to the eighteenth, Śaṅkara's voice was only one of many, and not an especially prominent one. He can in no way be held up as having spoken for all Indians, nor even all Hindus, nor even yet all Vedāntic interpreters of the Upaniṣads. Nor, indeed, was *his* Advaita Vedānta universally accepted among other Advaita Vedāntins. How, then, was it possible for Pessoa to arrive at the opinion that his view represents a pan-Indian ideal? Śaṅkara's elevation in the nineteenth century was largely the product of nationalist and nativist forces within India that sought in his work materials to counter the intellectual hegemony of the colonial West. Vivekananda (1863–1902), for example, would call upon Indians to "rouse and agitate the country with the lion-roar of Avaitavāda. Then I shall know you to be a Vedantist. First open a Sanskrit school there and teach the Upaniṣads and the Brahma-Sutras. Teach the boys the system of Brahmacharya" (Vivekananda [1902] 1972, 256–257). As Tapan Raychaudhuri has put it in his study of nineteenth-century attitudes, "The emerging nationalist consciousness adopted the heritage of the Hindu culture as the focus of its identity and glorified in the Hindu past. . . . Even the secular-agnostic trend in Bengali middle class culture, traceable back to the early days of the Hindu College—if not to the even older tradition of Navyanyāya—was subsumed by the ill-defined sense of national identity built around the Hindu heritage and its social body. A selective veneration for elements of the Hindu culture was thus the cultural bed-rock of the nationalist awareness" (Raychaudhuri 1988, 3). In the "selective veneration" of the illusionist metaphysics of Śaṅkara, Indian nationalists found the perfect vehicle with which to oppose what they perceived as the materialism and mercantilism of their British and Portuguese oppressors. This was just another imaginary India, and Pessoa cannot be blamed for having subscribed to a narrative just as eagerly consumed by the European Indologists of his time.

Pessoa and the Upaniṣads

When Pessoa quotes directly from the Upaniṣads, and not via the distorting lens of Śaṅkarite appropriation, his reading is more nuanced. He does so in this remarkable passage:

> It is difficult, of course, to understand what is meant by Union with God, but some idea may be given of what it is intended to mean. If we assume that, whatsoever may have been (apart from the falseness of using a tense, which implies time) the manner of God's creation of the world, the substance of that creation was the conversion by God of His own consciousness into the plural consciousness of separate beings. The great cry of the Indian Deity, "Oh that I might be many!" gives the idea without the idea of reality. (Pessoa 1985, 77)

Here Pessoa is quoting a line from the Chāndogya Upaniṣad: "And it thought to itself: 'Let me become many'" (Chāndogya Upaniṣad 6.2.3; Olivelle 1998, 247). Pessoa presumably encountered this line in the course of his reading of theosophical literature. Pessoa spent a good deal of time in 1915 and 1916 translating theosophical works into Portuguese, including Annie Besant's *Os ideaes da theosophia*, Helena Blavatsky's *A voz do silencio*, Mabel Collins' *Luz sobre o caminho e o karma*, and C. W. Leadbeater's *Compêndio de theosophia: a clarividência* e *auxiliares invisíveis* (for details, see Mota 2016, 235); he also, in 1922 and under the pseudonym Fernando de Castro, published a translation of a book by Besant from 1908, *Introduction to Yoga (Introdução ao Yoga)*.

Indeed, we find the very phrase that Pessoa quotes in Besant's *Wisdom of the Upanishads*, a 1907 title that Pessoa includes in a handwritten list of works published by the Theosophical Publishing Society in London (see Pizzaro, Ferrari, and Cardiello 2011, 171).

Besant writes with colour and flourish, and in her interpretation, what the Upaniṣads are given to say is this:

> There is no source of life save the Self, and only as He makes Himself identical with His emanation is it possible for a Universe to exist. As He affirms, there the Universe is; as He denies, the Universe vanishes into Him. This changing process, this thinking, "Let me be many," and then "Let the many cease," this is the continually recurring birth and death of Universes, and it is this triplicity, the Self, the Not-Self, and the Relation between them, which is summed up in the triple syllable, Aum.
>
> The appearance of a Universe and its disappearance, the succession in space and time, is that by which alone the eternal simultaneity of the Be-ness of the One can be expressed. The words I quoted from the *Chhâṇḍogyopaniṣhaṭ* are repeated in the *Taiṭṭirîyopaniṣhaṭ*: "He wished: 'May I be many, may I be born.'" He, the Supreme Îshvara, by the expression of His will became the many; He brought about first the duality between Himself and Mâyâ—He "wished a second . . . He divided"—and continuing that same thought of multiplicity, He limited and limited and limited Himself, until the infinite multiplicity of the Universe was made visible. The limitations are imposed by His will. He, the One, wills to be many, and the many depend on the forthgoing of that will to multiply. . . .
>
> What is Mâyâ? . . . [W]e have in Mâyâ the essence of separateness, due to His will to be many, and His consequent limitations of Himself by His thought of multiplicity. (Besant 1907, 31–32)

Noting that the line also appears in the Taittirīya Upaniṣad, Besant renders it as "May I be many" (Taittirīya 2.6; Olivelle [1998, 305] translates it as "He had this desire: 'Let me multiply myself'"). She here provides an exegesis of the Upaniṣads quite unlike that of Śaṅkara. It is one in which the multiplicity of the world is real, the result of *brahman* willing to multiply himself. According to Besant, what the Upaniṣads claim is that *brahman*, the "universal self," and individual human beings, "particular selves," are, as she puts it, "identical in nature":

> And that Brahma-viḍyâ, what is it? It is the central truth of the Upanişhaṭs. It is the identity in nature of the Universal and the Particular Self; *Ṭaṭ ṭvam asi*, THAT thou art. Such is the final truth, such the goal of all wisdom, of all devotion, of all right activity: THAT thou art. Nothing less than that is the Wisdom of the Upanişhaṭs; nothing more than that—for more than that there is not. That is the last truth of all truths; that is the final experience of all experiences. (Besant 1907, 3)

In Besant's reading there is no trace of the "Indian ideal." Individual human lives, being "identical in nature" with *brahman*, are therefore quite as real as *brahman*. Indeed, the view we find in this reading is rather similar to Pessoa's own in his hermetic and occult writings. Continuing the earlier quote, Pessoa writes:

> Union with God means therefore the repetition by the Adept of the Divine Act of Creation, by which he is identical with God in act, or manner of act, but, at the same time, an inversion of the Divine Act, by which he is still divided from God, or God's opposite, else he were God Himself and no union were required. The Adept, if he succeeds in making his consciousness one with the consciousness of all things, in making it an unconsciousness (or unselfconsciousness) which is conscious, repeats within himself the Divine Act, which is the conversion of God's individual consciousness into God's plural consciousness in individuals. (Pessoa 1985, 77)

Pessoa's marvellous phrase, "the conversion of God's individual consciousness into God's plural consciousness in individuals," can be paraphrased as stating that a divine self is transformed into a plurality of individual selves, a transformation that renders those individual selves "identical with God in act" without, of course, entailing the dissolution of God in the process. Whether identical in nature, as with Besant, or identical in act, as with Pessoa, the basic metaphysics is realist, and not the illusionist idealism that is Pessoa's "Indian ideal." Pessoa's relationship with Theosophy was, as is well known, complicated. Putting his thoughts now in the voice of the heteronym Raphael Baldaya, he does indeed see in it an expression of Indian ideas: "Theosophy, after all, is but a system of Indian philosophy that, by its vague and broad character, adapts itself perfectly to modern science, as it would adapt itself if by chance it was precisely the reverse, with respect to the principles upon which it was based" (AP 4047). This is the only occurrence of the phrase "Indian philosophy" I have yet to discover in his writings. Yet, on the other hand, he strongly disliked what he viewed as Theosophy's tendency towards "Christianization." Writing again as Baldaya, and intending to quote directly from Besant, he says:

> Recently, the propaganda of the religion known as Theosophy has gained a great [level of] prominence around the world. . . . Theosophists invoke the intimate continuity of the hermetic or esoteric tradition. According to a study of the literature connected to the exposition, purposefully confused, of the theories that formed the metaphysical base of the secret societies like the Rosa-Cruz . . . (quote here the due part of the *Ideals of Theosophy*) . . . Unfortunately, this study revealed fundamental principles that, regardless of their symbolic meaning, do not marry in any way with the theosophical theorizations. . . . Theosophy, as is appropriate and expected of our time, is only a democratization of hermeticism. If you want, it's a Christianization of it. (AP 4035)

Christianity is, again here as in his remarks about imperialism, accused of introducing an alien egalitarianism.

Even without the detour via Theosophy, however, it is evident that in directly quoting from the Upaniṣads Pessoa has available to him a richer perspective on Indian philosophy than the promulgation of the "Indian ideal" would otherwise have confined him to. It is significant that he feels no hesitation or embarrassment in quoting a line from the Chāndogya Upaniṣad in support of his own hermeticist view. When he adds that this line "gives the idea without the idea of reality" this is, presumably, evidence of the shadow that the "Indian ideal" still casts in his mind.

Pessoa's Indian Peers

Pessoa does not find the so-called Indian ideal an attractive one. He calls it "inhuman" and speaks of "the principle, which we already know to be absurd, that the universe is an illusion" (quoted in Lopes 1990, 394). The irony is that many early twentieth-century Indian intellectuals agreed with his rejection of this principle, extrapolated in a rarefied form from the philosophy of Śaṅkara. Among Pessoa's contemporaries were several extremely brilliant philosophers living and working in India who developed new interpretations of cardinal Advaita claims. The philosopher Jonathan Schaffer importantly distinguishes between what he calls "priority" and "existence" versions of monism, priority monism being the thesis that there is just one basic, foundational object grounding every other, existence monism claiming more strongly that this basic object is the one and only concrete object in existence (Schaffer 2010, 65). These new Advaita philosophers appreciated the point and distanced their interpretations from popular idealism. One such thinker is Aurobindo Ghose (1872–1950), someone who, like Pessoa, was critical of much that the Theosophical Society stood for. Aurobindo's withering criticism of this society was that, institutionally and doctrinally, it itself perfectly embodied cultural imperialism (Aurobindo [1910–1912] 1997, 67]. Another was

Anukulchandra Mukerji (1888–1968). Writing in Allahabad in 1938, in his seminal book *The Nature of Self*, Mukerji says:

> The conclusion we have tried to defend in the foregoing pages may be summarized as follows. All knowledge and experience [appertaining to individual human subjects] has for its ultimate implication an absolutely identical, eternal, infinite, unobjectifiable experience which may be called foundational experience. . . . If the terms "self" and "consciousness" be used, as they are very often used in modern philosophy, in the sense of a relation, then the foundational consciousness cannot be either a self or consciousness. But we have found ample reason to call it consciousness presupposed by all knowledge-events or fragmentary consciousness. (Mukerji 1938, 159, 236)

Mukerji is clear that this affirmation of priority monism is logically separable from the idealistic and absolutist thesis that nothing other than consciousness exists:

> A word of explanation may be useful at this place in regard to the precise meaning in which consciousness is said to be the *prius* of reality. This doctrine is often interpreted on the idealistic line and supposed to deny the independent existence of the material world apart from consciousness. This, however, would be to raise a highly controversial and difficult problem, and if the priority of consciousness could not be established till the age-long controversy on the relation between the external world and the knowing mind had been settled once and for all in favour of idealism, the Advaita theory of consciousness would naturally stand on a shaky foundation. It is, therefore, important to disassociate the assertion of the priority of consciousness from the idealistic contention and realise clearly that the doctrine of the priority of consciousness is equally compatible with the realistic belief in an independent world. (Mukerji 1938, 159, 113–114)

Mukerji was not alone in seeking to provide interpretations of Vedānta that distanced themselves from the mythology of the "Indian ideal." Surendranath Dasgupta was another, writing that "[*māyā*] has often been misinterpreted in the sense that all is pure and simple illusion . . . This is however a mistake, though one school does interpret Vedānta from this point of view. The Vedānta as explained by most of its illustrious exponents and particularly those whom I am following here, holds that things are as they are perceived" (Dasgupta 1941, 241). Sarvepalli Radhakrishnan, too, whose thought I will discuss in greater detail in Chapter 8, is emphatic in his dismissal of what he calls a "familiar criticism" of Hindu thought: "The two familiar criticisms that for Hindu thought the world is an illusion (*māyā*), that it is divine (pantheism) cancel each other. . . . For the Hindu thinkers, the objective world exists. It is not an illusion. It is real not in being ultimate, but in being a form, an expression of the ultimate" (Radhakrishnan 1936, 28). These non-idealist interpretations of the concept of *māyā* are very much in keeping with the argument I presented in the chapters of this book. As we saw in our discussion of K. C. Bhattacharyya above, there was a strong tendency among Pessoa's philosophical peers in India to reject the nativist quest for an ideal that is truly and uniquely "Indian," and instead to seek an "accommodation" between Indian and European philosophy that is free from mythologizing and idealization. So, to borrow a concept from Nietzsche studies, there is an "ironic affinity" (Morisson 1999) between a view Pessoa sometimes espouses as his own, in contrast with the "Indian ideal," and the ideas of his peers in the India he never knew.

8

"One Intellectual Breeze"

The idea that the universe itself is conscious, and indeed that we are its heteronyms, gives a new and profound meaning to the slogan "Be plural like the universe!" The slogan is now nothing but a repetition of the divinity's oath, "Let me become many!" Pessoa says, as we saw in Chapter 7, that "the great cry of the Indian Deity, 'Oh that I might be many!' gives the idea without the idea of reality" (Pessoa 1985, 77). God is here taken to be a universal, or cosmic, consciousness (*brahman*) of which every individual (*ātman*) is a heteronym.

Cosmic Consciousness: Whitman, Carpenter

To speak nowadays of cosmic consciousness, however, is to run the risk of inviting ridicule. Here's an example from a recent blog post, relating an anecdote told of the early pioneer of Sanskrit computational linguistics, Pandit Lakshimtatacharya: "My first encounter with Pt. Lakshimtatacharya was in Bangalore in about 1994, when we both attended a talk about libraries and manuscripts. After a speaker gave a somewhat inflated talk, starting with manuscripts and ending with *samādhi* and cosmic consciousness, a tall, imposing and very orthodox-looking Brāhmaṇa rose in the audience and said, 'Yes, it may well be as you say. But how are you able to distinguish what you have just described from a random, subjective neurological event?' My jaw fell open. It was obviously friendship from that moment on" (Wujastyk 2021). It was not always thus. William James, the illustrious Harvard philosopher, felt no shame in speaking of cosmic consciousness. In *The Varieties of Religious*

Fernando Pessoa. Jonardon Ganeri, Oxford University Press. © Oxford University Press 2024.
DOI: 10.1093/oso/9780197636688.003.0009

Experience, he wrote with praise of "a highly interesting volume" by the "Canadian psychiatrist, Dr. R. M. Bucke, [who] gives to the more distinctly characterized of these phenomena the name of cosmic consciousness" (James 1902, 389–390). James is speaking about Richard Maurice Bucke (1837–1902), sometime head of the Asylum for the Insane in London, Ontario, who did indeed write a book entitled *Cosmic Consciousness: A Study in the Evolution of the Human Mind*. Published in 1901, it sought to establish the reality of cosmic consciousness, which Bucke defines as "a higher form of consciousness than that possessed by the ordinary man . . . [one whose] prime characteristic . . . is, as its name implies, a consciousness of the cosmos, that is, of the life and order of the universe" (Bucke 1901, 2–3), which the book does by describing a diverse list of previous historical individuals who have experienced the phenomenon in question. Bucke would later reminisce that he "wrote a book in which he sought to embody the teaching of the illumination," adding, in an allusion to James, that "some who read it thought very highly of it" (1901, 9–10).

And yet, while his eponymous work did much to popularise it, it wasn't Bucke who invented the phrase. The inventor was the remarkable Englishman Edward Carpenter (1844–1929), a socialist, philosopher, and prescient activist for gay rights and prison reform. As a junior fellow of Trinity Hall Cambridge in 1880 or 1881, Carpenter had already befriended Ponnambalam Arunachalam (1853–1924), who would later become an illustrious Sri Lankan Tamil lawyer and receive a knighthood for his work in the Sri Lankan civil service. Arunachalam gave the impressionable Carpenter a copy of the *Bhagavad-gītā*, and a decade later invited him to visit Sri Lanka and India (Carpenter 1916, 250–253). Carpenter would later publish a selection of Arunachalam's letters as *Light from the East: Being Letters on Gñānam the Divine Knowledge by P. Arunachalam* (1923). Carpenter documented his formative trip in a travelogue entitled *From Adam's Peak to Elephanta: Sketches in Ceylon and India* (1892), and again in his autobiography, *My Days and Dreams* (1916). While Carpenter's descriptions of his travels reveal him to be a deeply humane and sympathetic observer, one who is often shocked and appalled by the abusive behaviour and attitudes of the British in India (I'm less sure that Bucke was similarly attuned to the situation in Canada), the most important event for us, and the principal reason for his visit, were the two months spent in Colombo sitting at the feet of one Ramaswami, an Indian sage and disciple of Tilleinathan Swami, and someone to whom Carpenter mostly refers to simply as "Gñāni," the savant. What Carpenter learns from Ramaswami is that what human beings seek "is a new order of consciousness—to which for want of a better word we may give the name *universal* or *cosmic* consciousness, in contradistinction to the individual or special bodily consciousness with which we are all familiar" (1892, 154).

With admirable honesty Carpenter admits that "I am not aware that the exact equivalent of this expression 'universal consciousness' is used in the Hindu philosophy; but the *Sat-Chit-ānanda Brahm* to which every yogi aspires indicates the same idea: *sat*, the reality, the all pervading; *chit*, the knowing, perceiving; *ānanda*, the blissful—all these united in one manifestation of Brahm" (ibid.). So the phrase "cosmic consciousness," as Carpenter introduces it, designates a "new order" of consciousness, corresponding in intent with the Hindu conception of *brahman* as bliss. Carpenter would later offer *jñāna-ākāśa* as a suitable Sanskrit equivalent, and, indeed, one must suspect that Ramaswami is channelling the *Mokṣopāya*, under its name *Yogavāsiṣṭha*, when he goes on to clarify that

> the true quality of the soul . . . is that of space, by which it is at rest, everywhere. But this space (*ākāsa*) within the soul is far above the ordinary material space. The whole of the latter, including all the suns and stars, appears to you then, as it were, but an atom of the former . . . [so that] this consciousness of space—not the material

> space, but the space within the soul—is a form of the supreme consciousness in man, the *sat-cit-ānanda* Brahm—Freedom, Equality, Extension, Omnipresence—and is accompanied by a sense which has been often described as a combination of all the senses—sight, hearing, touch, etc.—in one. (1892, 159, 188)

There is, incidentally, little doubt that the *Mokṣopāya* would have been well known; its content was in wide circulation, translated both into Hindi and into Persian several times for the Mughal court (Nair 2020). Arindam Chakrabarti reports that "for many years he heard the stories of the *Yogavāsiṣṭha* whispered late into the night in the ashram where he resided near Rishikesh" (Chapple and Chakrabarti 2015, xii). Carpenter's psychological makeup, however, made it obligatory for him to believe that he was receiving wisdom directly from an enlightened genius.

The sense in which consciousness is cosmic, then, is that it carries a universalizing phenomenology, and that what it feels like to be in such a state is to have a sense of all-encompassing spaciousness. This is, Carpenter will say in his autobiography, "the intense consciousness (not conviction merely) of the oneness of all life" (1892, 143). There is no suggestion in Carpenter that what the phrase "cosmic consciousness" refers to is the idea that the cosmos itself is conscious. The phrase is exclusively associated with a plane of phenomenology in which "individual self and life thin away to a mere film, and are only the shadows cast by the glory revealed beyond" (1892, 155). As he formulates it in his introduction to his edition of the letters of Arunachalam, "*Gñana-akaśa* is (as the very juxtaposition of the two words would seem to imply) . . . the knowledge which *is* space. It is the identification of space with consciousness. It is the medium within which Thought may indeed move, but which far surpasses all Thought and imagination in the width and swiftness of its embrace" (1923, 21).

Carpenter claims, and I find this to be the most extraordinary part of the whole story, that his encounter with Ramaswami is what led him to a new defence of democracy. Already in his travelogue he writes:

> This was one of the most remarkable parts of the Guru's teaching. Though (for family reasons) maintaining many of the observances of Caste himself, and though holding and teaching that for the mass of the people caste rules were quite necessary, he never ceased to insist that when the time came for a man (or woman) to be "emancipated" all these rules must drop aside as of no importance—all distinction of castes, classes, all sense of superiority or self-goodness—of right and wrong even—and the most absolute sense of Equality must prevail towards every one, and determination in its expression. Certainly it was remarkable (though I knew that the sacred books contained it) to find this germinal principle of Western democracy so vividly active and at work deep down beneath the innumerable layers of Oriental social life and custom. But so it is; and nothing shows better the relation between the West and the East than this fact.
>
> This sense of Equality, of Freedom from regulations and confinements, of Inclusiveness, and of the Life that "rests everywhere," belongs of course more to the cosmic or universal part of man than to the individual part. To the latter it is always a stumbling-block and an offence. It is easy to show that men are not equal, that they cannot be free, and to point the absurdity of a life that is indifferent and at rest under all conditions. Nevertheless to the larger consciousness these are basic facts, which underlie the common life of humanity, and feed the very individual that denies them.
>
> Thus repeating the proviso that in using such terms as cosmic and universal consciousness we do not commit ourselves to the theory that the instant a man leaves the personal part of him he enters into absolutely unlimited and universal knowledge, but only into a higher order of perception—and admitting the intricacy and complexity of the region so roughly denoted by these

> terms, and the microscopical character of our knowledge about it—we may say once more, also as a roughest generalisation, that the quest of the East has been this universal consciousness, and that of the West the personal or individual consciousness. (Carpenter 1892, 162–163)

The argument from cosmic consciousness to democracy as contained in this passage seems to be this: there is a "higher order of perception" in which the various differences between individuals are not phenomenologically manifest, and to such a state of consciousness all people are equal because no inequality is apparent.

In 1883, Carpenter published a volume of poetry in the style of one of Pessoa's heroes, Walt Whitman, and which he calls *Towards Democracy*. Incidentally, Whitman's debt to the philosophies of classical India, most especially to the *Bhagavad-gītā*, despite certain efforts to suppress it, has been well chronicled (e.g., Rajasekharaiah 1970): the chain is from India to Whitman and from Whitman to Pessoa. The circle is closed with Carpenter, for thanks to his volume of poetry Carpenter's name was known even to Aurobindo, Gandhi, and Tagore. It was known too to Pessoa, who mentions Carpenter as a potential recipient of a copy of his *English Poems* (Zenith 2021, 729).

Carpenter explains his motivation in an essay for the newspaper *The Labour Prophet*. In the lead-up to writing *Towards Democracy*, he says, he

> became for the first time overwhelmingly conscious of the disclosure within me of a region transcending in some sense the ordinary bounds of personality, in the light of which region my own idiosyncrasies of character—defects, accomplishments, limitations, or what not—appeared of no importance whatever—an absolute freedom from mortality, accompanied by an indestructible calm and joy. I immediately saw, or felt, that this region of self existing in me existed equally (though not always equally

> consciously) in others. In regard to it the mere diversities of temperament which ordinarily distinguish and divide people dropped away and became indifferent, and a field was opened in which all might meet, in which all were truly equal. Thus the two words which controlled my thought and expression at that time became Freedom and Equality. (Carpenter 1894)

Cosmic consciousness has become a sense of our common humanity. In *Civilization: Its Cause and Cure*, Carpenter speaks of "the delusion that man can exist for himself alone—his outer and, as it were, accidental self apart from the great inner and cosmical self by which he is one with his fellows" (1889, 52). Commenting on his use of the authorial first person, Carpenter strikes a remarkably Pessoan tone:

> It seems to me more and more clear that the word "I" has a practically infinite range of meaning—that the ego covers far more ground than we usually suppose. At some points we are intensely individual, at others intensely sympathetic; some of our impressions (as the tickling of a hair) are of the most momentary character, others (as the sense of identity) involve long periods of time. Sometimes we are aware of almost a fusion between our own identity and that of another person. What does all this mean? Are we really separate individuals, or is individuality an illusion, or, again, is it only a part of the ego or soul that is individual and not the whole? . . . Anyhow, what am I? (Carpenter 1894)

In *Towards Democracy* it is the voice of the cosmic self that is speaking: "So I am the space within the soul, of which the space without is but the similitude and mental image; / Comest thou to inhabit me, thou hast the entrance to all life—death shall no longer divide thee from whom thou lovest" (1883, 343). According to Carpenter, then, there is a region, field, or space (Skt. *ākāśa*) within human subjectivity and self-awareness in which individual personality is transcended, meaning that differences of individual character are felt as insignificant and the separateness between individuals is felt to be an artefact. This region, which can be accessed by everybody, grounds a sense of our common humanity and our equality. He finds this idea in the teachings of Ramaswami as in the poems of Walt Whitman, who was himself, as is well known, influenced by his readings of Hindu scripture.

Let me sum up what we have learnt from our brief history of the phrase "cosmic consciousness." We have discovered that this phrase serves as stand-in for the doctrine we might call psychological monism. Psychological monism is the phenomenological thesis that there is a mode of consciousness in which everything is experienced as being one with everything else, and that this mode of consciousness (of the cosmos as a single whole) can serve to provide prima facie justification for a range of egalitarian and cosmopolitan beliefs, such as the belief that everyone, as members of a common humanity, is equal. Psychological monism belongs to the type of theory according to which experience supplies prima facie justification for belief: just as my perceptual experience as of a table before me justifies, in the absence of defeaters, my belief that there is a table here, so too my cosmic experience, my experience as of the cosmos being a single whole, justifies my belief in the equal standing of all humanity.

The idea that the universal consciousness of Advaita Vedānta should lead to a common fellowship among mankind would find another vociferous advocate in Sarvepalli Radhakrishnan. His inaugural lecture on assuming the Spalding Chair in Eastern Religions and Ethics, which he entitled *The World's Unborn Soul* and delivered at Oxford University in October 1936, is exemplary. Radhakrishnan begins by pointing out that the world of 1936 is in a state of crisis, one of fragmented nationalism. Every civilization, he claims, is an experiment in living. But the European experiment has reached a dead end, its only hope of salvation lying with an infusion of ideas from India. For, as he puts it, it would be "an academic error, a failure of perspective," for Europeans not to listen to sources of inspiration found in the world's literature. "Perhaps, the civilizations of the East, their religions and ethics, may offer us some help in negotiating difficulties we are up against. . . . Now that we have the whole world for our cultural base, the process of discovery and training in classics cannot cease with listening to the voices of Isaiah and Paul, Socrates and Cicero" (Radhakrishnan 1936, 1). Mankind, Radhakrishnan says, is still in the making. It has the potential for universal fellowship, a common humanity based on a shared form of subjectivity. And this is, famously, Radhakrishnan's fundamental idea: that there is a common, universal core in the subjective character of all human experience, a commonality that represents the best of us and on which a universal feeling of camaraderie can be based. His is a conception of authenticity based on rediscovery of this basal core of universal subjectivity:

> The aim of all human living is self-definition. It is to isolate the substantial permanence which each finite life possesses deep down, from the strife of empirical happenings. We can exceed the limits within which human consciousness normally functions. Man can abstract from his body and flesh, from his feelings and desires, even from thoughts which rise like waves on the surface of his mind, and reach a pure awareness, *the naked condition of his pure selfhood.* (1936, 26; italics added)

"What is our true self?" Radhakrishnan asks, answering, "While our bodily organization undergoes changes, while our thoughts gather like clouds in the sky and disperse again, the self is never lost. It is present in all, yet distinct from all. Its nature is not affected by ordinary happenings. It is the source of the sense of identity through numerous transformations. It remains itself though it sees all things. . . . This persisting self which is universal seer to all things seen, this essential awareness which nothing has the power to suppress" (1936, 24). A self that is never lost, independent of the vagaries of our physiological and psychological constitution, an everpresent and unchanging source of self-awareness, represents, for Radhakrishnan, the ultimate ground of human fraternity.

Ironically, although "never lost," this self, as the Upaniṣadic seers were the first to discover, is remarkably hard to actually find. The new philosophical principle that emerges in Radhakrishnan's mind is that of intuition, "where intellect, will and emotion are fully integrated, and man is one with the spirit in him" (Datta 1948, 558). Rediscovering this pure, universal self, the "authentic being" from which we have become "exiled," is the solution we have been looking for, the solution to the problem of how to live in our age of insularity:

> The fundamental truths of a spiritual religion are that our real self is the supreme being, which it is our business to discover and consciously become, and this being is one in all. The soul that has found itself is no longer conscious of itself in its isolation. It is conscious rather of the universal life of which all individuals, races, and nations are specific articulations. . . . Those who are anxious to live in peace with their own species and all life will not find it possible to gloat over the massacres of large numbers of men simply because they do not belong to their race or country. . . . Our normal attitudes to other races and nations are no more than artificial masks, habits of thought and feeling, sedulously cultivated by long practice in dissimulation. . . . Racialism and nationalism which require us to exercise our base passions, to bully and cheat, to kill and loot, all with a feeling that we are profoundly virtuous and doing God's work, are abhorrent to the spiritually awakened. For them all races and nations lie beneath the same arch of heaven. They proclaim a new social relationship and serve a new society with civil liberties for all individuals, and political freedom for all nations great and small. (1936, 30)

Radhakrishnan does not himself employ the phrase "cosmic consciousness," but the continuity between his ideas and those of Carpenter is evident.

We may wonder how good, ultimately, the argument from cosmic consciousness to democracy really is. The argument evidently presupposes both that cosmic consciousness is veridical and that the absence of *perceived* distinctions entails the absence of *real* distinctions. Democracy, however, does surely require that there is a plurality of numerically distinct individuals, whereas to cosmic consciousness neither numerical nor qualitative distinctness is apparent. The argument seems on the face of it to be self-defeating. For it is a basic presupposition of any egalitarian belief that there is a plurality of distinct individual subjects, and yet this presupposition is inconsistent with the veridicality of the content of the cosmic experience, which is meant to supply the belief with justification. For this reason, I am sceptical of Carpenter's claim that cosmic consciousness provides democracy with political legitimacy, and of Radhakrishnan's analogous claim for internationalism and cosmopolitanism. The defenders of such claims seem to feel that they need only establish the existence of cosmic consciousness for their conclusion to follow, but what worries me is that there is a non sequitur in the deduction. More important than such caveats, however, is the way the story of this argument is entwined with a new attempt to provide socialism and democracy with a philosophical foundation. What our delving into its history has revealed is that the contemporary ridicule with which the phrase "cosmic consciousness" is met is quite misplaced: to the contrary, it has held a place of honour in important movements of democratic and internationalist social reform.

Is the Cosmos Conscious? Coleridge, James

The phrase "cosmic consciousness" has still more to offer an attentive interpreter. If as a subjective genitive it means a consciousness whose content is cosmic; as an objective genitive its meaning is a consciousness that pertains to the cosmos itself. So is the cosmos itself conscious? Let us backtrack. Bucke tells the story of his own first experiential encounter with cosmic consciousness. Writing of himself in the third person, he says:

> It was in the early spring, at the beginning of his thirty-sixth year. He and two friends had spent the evening reading Wordsworth, Shelley, Keats, Browning, and especially Whitman. They parted at midnight, and he had a long drive in a hansom (it was in an English city). His mind, deeply under the influence of the ideas, images and emotions called up by the reading and talk of the evening, was calm and peaceful. He was in a state of quiet, almost passive enjoyment. All at once, without warning of any kind, he found himself wrapped around as it were by a flame-colored cloud. For an instant he thought of fire, some sudden conflagration in the great city; the next, he knew that the light was within himself. Directly afterwards came upon him a sense of exultation, of immense joyousness accompanied or immediately followed by an intellectual illumination quite impossible to describe. Into his brain streamed one momentary lightning-flash of the Brahmic Splendor which has ever since lightened his life; upon his heart fell one drop of Brahmic Bliss, leaving thenceforward for always an aftertaste of heaven. Among other things he did not come to believe, he saw and knew that the Cosmos is not dead matter but a living Presence, that the soul of man is immortal, that the universe is so built and ordered that without any peradventure all things work together for the good of each and all, that the foundation principle of the world is what we call love and that the happiness of every one is in the long run absolutely certain. (Bucke 1901, 9–10)

In equivocating between his official definition of cosmic consciousness as "a higher form of consciousness" in human beings and the different meaning in which what is affirmed is that the cosmos is "not dead matter but a living presence," Bucke effectively confuses psychological monism with cosmopsychism. Cosmopsychism is a special case of the metaphysical view that Jonathan Schaffer, in his essay entitled "Monism," calls "priority monism," the view that the whole is a fundamental reality whose constituent parts are grounded in it (Schaffer 2010). As already pointed out in Chapter 7, Schaffer distinguishes between what he calls "priority" and "existence" versions of monism, priority monism being the thesis that there is just one basic, foundational object grounding every other, existence monism claiming, more strongly, that this basic object is the one and only concrete object in existence. Cosmopsychists who do not deny the existence of a plurality of conscious individual subjects of experience but regard them as metaphysically grounded in the basic foundational consciousness that is cosmic consciousness are priority rather than existence monists, in this sense. William James, when he again invokes the phrase "cosmic consciousness" in a 1909 essay, "The Confidences of a Psychical Researcher," uses it in precisely in this second sense. He writes:

> My own dramatic sense tends instinctively to picture the situation as an interaction between slumbering faculties in the automatist's mind and a cosmic environment of *other consciousness* of some sort which is able to work upon them. If there were in the universe a lot of diffuse soul-stuff, unable of itself to get into consistent personal form, or to take permanent possession of an organism, yet always craving to do so, it might get its head into the air, parasitically, so to speak, by profiting by weak spots in the armor of human minds, and slipping in and stirring up there the sleeping tendency to personate. It would induce habits in the subconscious region of the mind it used thus, and would seek above all things to prolong its social opportunities by making itself agreeable and plausible. It would drag stray scraps of truth with it from the wider environment, but would betray its mental

> inferiority by knowing little how to weave them into any important or significant story. (2001, 155)

Noting that this view "has the advantage of falling into line with ancient human traditions," James writes:

> Out of my experience, such as it is (and it is limited enough) one fixed conclusion dogmatically emerges, and that is this, that we with our lives are like islands in the sea, or like trees in the forest. The maple and the pine may whisper to each other with their leaves, and Conanicut and Newport hear each other's foghorns. But the trees also commingle their roots in the darkness underground, and the islands also hang together through the ocean's bottom. Just so there is a continuum of cosmic consciousness, against which our individuality builds but accidental fences, and into which our several minds plunge as into a mother-sea or reservoir. Our "normal" consciousness is circumscribed for adaptation to our external earthly environment, but the fence is weak in spots, and fitful influences from beyond leak in, showing the otherwise unverifiable common connection. Not only psychic research, but metaphysical philosophy, and speculative biology are led in their own ways to look with favor on some such "panpsychic" view of the universe as this. Assuming this common reservoir of consciousness to exist, this bank upon which we all draw, and in which so many of earth's memories must in some way be stored, or mediums would not get at them as they do, the question is, What is its own structure? What is its inner topography? This question, first squarely formulated by Myers, deserves to be called "Myers's problem" by scientific men hereafter. What are the conditions of individuation or insulation in this mother-sea? To what tracts, to what active systems functioning separately in it, do personalities correspond? Are individual "spirits" constituted there? Now numerous, and of how many hierarchic orders may these then be? How permanent?

> How transient? And how confluent with one another may they become? ([1909] 2007, 155–156)

The cosmos is conscious. It is not itself personal but has a "will to personate," a craving to consolidate itself into individual persons. This is, of course, not "will" in the normal sense of a personal will, but rather in the same sense in which James refers to a "will to believe," a subpersonal force below the level of personal belief and desire. When James asks, "To what tracts, to what active systems functioning separately in it, do personalities correspond?," he is raising, perhaps for the first time, a difficult problem for cosmopsychism. His solution, barely hinted at, is that there is a process of condensation to which he gives the name "will to personate."

The difficulty for impersonal varieties of cosmopsychism, such as this one, is to see how the impersonal consciousness exhibited by the cosmos can possibly be the right sort of thing to serve as metaphysical ground for the consciousness exhibited by individual subjects of experience. This cosmic consciousness is the impersonal bed out of which individual subjects of experience nucleate and distil. How, though, can that which is fundamentally impersonal ever serve as a metaphysical ground for that which is fundamentally personal? Cosmopsychists have reached for a range of metaphors, from James' "will to personate" to talk inspired by contemporary physics. But the "explanatory gap" remains, and this is cosmopsychism's own "hard problem."

The Romantic poet Samuel Taylor Coleridge (1772–1834), who was also in his own way an avid philosopher, advances a proposal along similar lines to that of James in his famous poem "Effusion XXXV," later renamed "The Eolian Harp":

> And what if all of animated nature
> Be but organic Harps diversely framed,
> That tremble into Thought, as o'er them sweeps

> Plastic and vast, one intellectual breeze,
> At once the soul of each, and God of all? (2009, II:36–40)

The metaphor deployed here is that of a single wind that shakes into motion a multiplicity of organic bodies, "one intellectual breeze" that "trembles into Thought" each and every individual human organism. As Coleridge put it in a line he later redacted, "And each one's Tubes be that, which each calls I." That is Coleridge's claim to belong with the premodern poets of plurality I discussed in Chapter 1, alongside Keats and Hazlitt's Shakespeare. But in the redaction lies the rub, for it is unclear how a psychological trembling brought on by a breeze of consciousness could ever result in a subject of experience with a uniquely first-personal perspective, a for-me-ness unshared by the "intellectual breeze" itself.

The assumption of James and Coleridge is that when the phrase is construed objectively, cosmic consciousness is impersonal. Confronted with the decomposition problem, however, a cosmopsychist seems to have no choice but to affirm that cosmic consciousness is itself a subject of experience, an "I" with a uniquely first-personal perspective. That, certainly, was how Ralph Waldo Emerson (1803–1882) took the idea, writing in a famous 1841 essay—with which Bucke was certainly familiar—of an "over-soul within which every man's particular being is contained and made one with all other" and, again, that "within man is the soul of the whole; the wise silence; the universal beauty, to which every part and particle is equally related, the eternal ONE. And this deep power in which we exist and whose beatitude is all accessible to us, is not only self-sufficing and perfect in every hour, but the act of seeing and the thing seen, the seer and the spectacle, the subject and the object, are one. We see the world piece by piece, as the sun, the moon, the animal, the tree; but the whole, of which these are shining parts, is the soul" (Emerson 2000, 237). The suggestion here is that individual selves are parts of a single larger whole self. It is well known that Emerson had deeply immersed himself in the *Bhagavad-gītā*, and indeed there are passages in the *Gītā* in which Kṛṣṇa likens himself to an oversoul (for Emerson's influence on Pessoa, see Zavatta 2021). More particularly, Kṛṣṇa seems to articulate a version of priority monism when he describes individual selves as his own parts: "Just a fragment [*aṃśa*] of me in the realm of the living is the permanent individual self" (*Gītā* 15.7). It is, needless to say, a very large step in Hindu theology to identify the Kṛṣṇa of the *Bhagavad-gītā* with the *brahman* of the Upaniṣads. This was the move taken by the theologian Śaṅkara in his commentaries on both bodies of scripture, and for many of the European authors who were exposed to Hindu literature in the nineteenth century, through encounters exactly like that between Carpenter and Ramaswami, Śaṇkara's monistic Advaita Vedānta was what they understood Hinduism to be. It has been argued that Coleridge too was influenced by the *Bhagavad-Gītā*, which he read in Wilkins' 1785 translation (see Srivastava 2002, 216, 222–226, referring especially to *Gītā* 7.5–7: "My material nature is eightfold, comprising the order of earth, water, fire, wind, ether, mind, spirit, and ego. This is my lower nature but know that I have another, higher nature which comprises the order of souls: it is by the latter that this world is sustained, strong-armed prince. Realize that all creatures have their source therein: I am the origin of this entire universe and its dissolution" [van Buitenen 1981, 99]). That Coleridge had read of Advaita Vedānta is evident from a marginal inscription in his copy of Dubois' 1817 *Description of the Character, Manners and Customs of the People of India*. There, in the margin of page 323, Coleridge describes Spinoza as "the sternest and most consistent of Adwitamists" (see Srivastava 2002, 209).

A Pessoan Cosmopsychism

And yet I don't agree that one can base the personal variety of cosmopsychism on the idea that the relation between the cosmic self and individual subjects of experience is mereological, for the simple reason that it makes no sense to say that one subject of experience is, literally, a part of another one, not least because individual psychological perspectives or points of view do not combine or decombine. It is in the writings of still another philosopher-poet that I find a more promising version of the personal variety of cosmopsychism. As we have seen in earlier chapters, Fernando Pessoa introduces the term of art "heteronymy" for the mental act of simulating one individual subject of experience within another. If a *pseudonym* is a mask, a disguise intended, even if perhaps only ironically, to hide the true identity of the author, a *heteronym* is something else entirely: it is the author writing "outside his own person" and in doing so transforming himself into another I. A heteronym occupies the first-person position within the experience of the author, and has a defined literary voice and a distinctive power of expression. So to write in the name of a heteronym is not to hide oneself behind a mask but to imagine living in experience as that very person: each heteronym, Pessoa says, is "lived by the author within himself" and has "passed through his soul" (2001, 2) A heteronym is "someone in me who has taken my place" (2002, #351).

In assuming a heteronym, one transforms oneself into another I: "First we must create another I, charged with suffering—in and for us—everything we suffer" (2002, 455). The experiences of my heteronym are both *in* me, in the sense that I am their host, and also *for* me, standing, with respect to me, in a first-personal subjective relationship. When Pessoa writes of heteronymy that it is a subjective state in which "every felt pain is automatically analysed to the core, ruthlessly foisted on an extraneous I" (2002, 456), he exactly formulates the essence of the concept in the idea of experience that is at once irreducibly first-personal and yet also alien. A heteronym is a fully formed subject subsisting within one's conscious experience.

Let me call the view that individual human subjects are heteronyms of a single higher-order self "heteronymic cosmopsychism" (see Ganeri 2021, 140). Heteronymic cosmopsychism is different from the variety of cosmopsychism in which the grounding relation between the single cosmic self and the multiplicity of individual selves is mereological, and which claims to ground individual selves by subsuming them in the cosmic self by decomposition (e.g., Goff 2017). The idea that the grounding relation is mereological creates, to repeat, serious difficulties. As Itay Shani and Joachim Keppler put it, "Part of what makes the subject constitution problem so intractable is that it has been shown to repeatedly involve serious conceptual *aporia*. . . . [M]ost, if not all, of these conceptual tangles appear to be related to the assumption that one perspectival subject is literally composed of, or fractured from, another. In the idiom of cosmopsychism, the assumption is that the cosmos itself is a universal mind and that all lesser minds partake in it like colored tiles cut from a jigsaw puzzle's cardboard model—each carrying about itself a small piece of the grand picture" (2018, 405). The point is that it makes no sense to claim that one can build a new subject that has several "smaller" subjects as its parts, nor to disaggregate a single subject into a cluster of "smaller" subjects. To do this would be like trying to take two distinct points of view of a scene and combine them to create a third point of view distinct from the original two. Pessoa himself records this fact in his wish "to be two kings at the same time: not the one soul of them both, but two distinct, kingly soul" (Pessoa 2002, #404).

What heteronymic cosmopsychism says, in contrast, is that there are multiple heteronyms of the fundamental cosmic self. Pessoa, well-read in Indian philosophy, quotes directly from the Upaniṣads, and his reading is nuanced. He does so in this remarkable text, to which I have already referred: "It is difficult, of course, to understand what is meant by Union with God, but some idea may be given of what it is intended to mean. If we assume that, whatsoever may have been (apart from the falseness of using a tense, which implies time) the manner of God's creation of the world, the substance of that creation was the conversion by God of His own consciousness into the plural consciousness of separate beings. The great cry of the Indian Deity, 'Oh that I might be many!' gives the idea without the idea of reality" (Pessoa 1985, 77). As I noted in Chapter 7, Pessoa is here quoting a line from the Chāndogya Upaniṣad: "And it thought to itself: 'Let me become many'" (Chāndogya Upaniṣad 6.2.3; Olivelle 1998, 247), Pessoa presumably having encountered this line in the course of his work translating the theosophical writings of Annie Besant.

So the philosophy of cosmic consciousness is actually two monisms under one heading. One is the epistemology of psychological monism, according to which a distinctive sort of "cosmic" experience supplies epistemic justification to egalitarian beliefs. The other is the metaphysics of cosmopsychism, which holds that the consciousness exhibited by the cosmos provides metaphysical grounding to the consciousness constitutive of individual subjects of experience. The interwoven story of these two monisms is entangled with the story of the nineteenth- and twentieth-century reception of Śaṅkara's monistic Advaita Vedānta in Europe, and with efforts in India to disentangle various strands within Hindu philosophical literature from their fusion in Śaṅkara's monistic system. I have said that I am sceptical of Carpenter's claim that cosmic consciousness provides democracy with political legitimacy, and of Radhakrishnan's analogous claim for internationalism and cosmopolitanism. The defenders of such claims seem to feel that those claims require only that the existence of cosmic consciousness is established, but their conclusion does not seem to follow. As for cosmopsychism, in its impersonal variety, according to which the consciousness of the cosmos is an impersonal mass of psychological stuff, the "hard problem" is that this does not seem to be the right sort of stuff to serve as metaphysical ground to individual subjects of experience, each with its own unique first-person perspective. I distinguish two versions of the personal variety of cosmopsychism, which has it that the consciousness of the cosmos is itself a subject of experience. One of these, which I trace to Emerson and before him to the *Bhagavad-gītā*, holds that the grounding relation is mereological, and runs afoul of the so-called decomposition problem. But I also detected, in the philosophical writings of two poets, Coleridge and Pessoa, evidence of another version, which isolates the grounding relation in the work of heteronymic simulation and the imagination. If the rhetoric of cosmic consciousness is to have any future in philosophy, then it seems that it must lie here.

Glossary

Avatāra. "Descent, alighting, descending or going down into" (Apte). A general expression to designate entities that come down to earth from some higher realm. Typically not merely re-embodied but as having a new bearing.

Bearing. An entire outlook, a way of being in the world; an emotional, cognitive and sensory landscape.

Cosmopsychism. The thesis that the cosmos as a whole displays psychological properties and that the mental states of human beings, and indeed human beings themselves as individual subjects of experience, are metaphysically grounded in the cosmopsychological properties of the cosmos.

***De se* imagining.** Imagining "from the inside" doing something or being someone doing something.

Depersonalization. Not that there is an imperson substrate of conscious experience, but that experiences are always felt as owned by another.

Dreaming. A virtual reality environment generated by the imagination.

Explicit *de se* imagining. Imagining oneself from an external, third person point of view. The subject must think of the object of his/her imagination as himself/herself, and must represent himself/herself from an objective point of view, that is, from outside.

Field-consciousness. A bedrock of consciousness that underwrites any way of seeing.

Forumnal self-awareness. To think of oneself as a "meeting-place" with no personality of its own is to think that there is a sort of self-awareness more primitive than that of having an individuated point of view.

Heteronymic cosmopsychism. The view that individual human subjects are heteronyms of a single higher-order self. A line from the Chāndogya Upaniṣad: "And it thought to itself: 'Let me become many.'"

Heteronym. An imagined mind, simulated self, subjective artefact, individuated point of view, and no less real for that. A heteronym occupies the first-person position within the experience of the author, and has a defined literary voice and a distinctive power of expression.

Heteronymy. Not merely having another name, but rather having the name of another; the mental act of simulating one individual subject of experience within another.

Highest Stage of Dreaming. When, having created a picture with various figures whose lives we live all at the same time, we are jointly and interactively all those souls. Imagining living multiple lives simultaneously in parallel.

Immersive centrality/positional conception of self. The idea that one inhabits a central perspective within the simulated field of experience.

Immersive for-me-ness. The idea that how one experiences matters as much as what one experiences.

"Indian ideal", the. The idea that the entire world is an illusion.

Intersectionism. The presence of objects in both of two fields of experience.

Intersubjective transference in imagination. Another name for heteronymy.

māyā. Not illusion, but rather "artistic power."

Mechanism of self-duplication. Pluralization by living a life in parallel.

Mechanism of self-estrangement. The subject of experience becomes, inside the virtual reality of a poem, another.

Memory asymmetry. The protagonist remembers nothing about his or her former life for as long as he or she is within the simulation, but clearly remembers the simulation life when outside it.

Mokṣopāya. A great Kashmiri philosophical storybook better known as the *Yogavāsiṣṭha.*

Poetry. Poetry is astonishment, an astonishment of the sort one feels on encountering something for the first time, and finding in everything thus encountered a "deeper meaning" that seems to stem from an indeterminate sense of familiarity. Poetry is admiration, a respect for the beauty of all that the world contains. A simultaneous attention to the sound and meaning of words.

Positional concept of the self. By virtue of occupying the subject position, a particular entity, a particular human being, is "me," the one that "I am."

Quasi-*de se* imagination. Remembering doing something but without self-attribution.

Reality++. The idea that there are virtual subjects as well as virtual objects, that by immersing oneself in a virtual reality generated by one's imagination one might also virtualize oneself.

Self. A way of feeling; a style of experiencing the world.

Trans-simulation object identity. The hypothesis that virtual objects, the objects within a simulation, are identical to normal objects, objects without the simulation.

Virtual realism. The view that virtual are just as real as other sorts of object.

Bibliography

Alford, Lucy. 2020. *Forms of Poetic Attention*. New York: Columbia University Press.

Amiel, Henri-Frédéric. (1885) 1889. *Amiel's Journal: The Journal Intime of Henri-Fréderic Amiel*. Translated by Mary A. Ward. New York: Macmillan. [Original title: *Fragments d'un journal intime*.]

AP. Arquivo Pessoa. http://arquivopessoa.net. [An archive of Pessoa's texts, fragments, and poetry.]

Aurobindo Ghose. [1910–1912] 1997. "The Claims of Theosophy." In *Essays Divine and Human: The Complete Works of Sri Aurobindo*, vol. 12. Pondicherry: Sri Aurobindo Ashram.

Benton, Richard P. 1966. "Keats and Zen." *Philosophy East and West* 16: 33–47.

Besant, Annie. 1907. *Wisdom of the Upanishads*. Madras: Theosophical Publishing House.

Bhattacharyya, Krishnachandra. [1931] 1954. "Swarāj in Ideas." *Visvabharati Quarterly* 20: 103–114.

Borges, Jorge Luis. 1999. *Collected Fictions*. Translated by Andrew Hurley. London: Penguin Books.

Bucke, Richard Maurice. *Cosmic Consciousness: A Study in the Evolution of the Human Mind*. Philadelphia: Innes & Sons, 1901.

Buitenen, J. A. B. van, trans. 1981. *The Bhagavadgītā in the Mahābhārata*. Chicago: University of Chicago Press.

Cardiello, Antonio, and Pietro Gori. 2016. "Nietzsche's and Pessoa's Psychological Fictionalism." *Pessoa Plural* 10: 578–605.

Carlsen, Robert S. 1997. *The War for the Heart and Soul of a Highland Maya Town*. Austin: University of Texas Press.

Carlson, Thomas A. 2008. *The Indiscrete Image: Infinitude and Creation of the Human*. Chicago: University of Chicago Press.

Carpenter, Edward. 1883. *Towards Democracy*. Manchester: Joh Heywood. [Part 1; three more parts in subsequent years.]

Carpenter, Edward. 1889. *Civilisation: Its Cause and Cure*. London: George Allen & Unwin.

Carpenter, Edward. 1892. *From Adam's Peak to Elephanta: Sketches in Ceylon and India*. London: George Allen & Unwin.

Carpenter, Edward. 1894. "Towards Democracy." *The Labour Prophet*, May 1894, 49–51.

Carpenter, Edward. 1916. *My Days and Dreams: Being Autobiographical Notes*. London: George Allen & Unwin.

Carpenter, Edward. 1927. "Introduction." In *Light from the East: Being Letters on Gñānam the Divine Knowledge by Hon. P. Arunachalam*, 9–30. London: George Allen & Unwin.

Chakrabarti, Arindam. 2015. "Is This a Dream? A Critique of the *Mokṣopāya*'s Take on Experience, Objecthood, and the 'External' World." In *Engaged Emancipation: Mind, Morals, and Make-Believe in the Mokṣopāya (Yogavāsiṣṭha)*, edited by Arindam Chakrabarti and Christopher Key Chapple, 79–96. Albany: State University of New York Press.

Chakrabarti, Arindam. 2018. "Dream, Death, and Death Within a Dream." In *Imaginations of Death and the Beyond in India and Europe*, edited by Günter Blamberger and Sudhir Kakar, 101–117. Singapore: Springer Singapore.

Chalmers, David. 2022. *Reality+: Virtual Worlds and the Problems of Philosophy*. New York: Norton.

Chapple, Christopher Key, and Chakrabarti, Arindam, eds. 2015. *Engaged Emancipation: Mind, Morals, and Make-Believe in the Mokṣopāya (Yogavāsiṣṭha)*. Albany: State University of New York Press.

Coleridge, Samuel Taylor. 2009. *The Major Works*. Oxford: Oxford University Press.

Couture, André. 2001. "From Viṣṇu's Deeds to Viṣṇu's Play, or Observations on the Word *Avatāra* as a Designation for the Manifestations of Viṣṇu." *Journal of Indian Philosophy* 29, no. 3: 313–326.

Couture, André. 2010. "Avatāra." In *Brill's Encyclopedia of Hinduism*, vol. 2, *Sacred Texts and Languages, Ritual Traditions, Arts, Concepts*, edited by Knut A. Jacobsen, 701–705. Leiden: Brill.

CSP. Casa Fernando Pessoa. http://bibliotecaparticular.casafernandopessoa.pt/index/aut/ index.htm. [Scans of the books in Pessoa's personal library with his marginal notes.]

Dasgupta, Surendranath. 1941. "Some Implications of Realism in the Vedānta Philosophy." In *Philosophical Essays*, 234–254. Calcutta: University of Calcutta.

Datta, Dhirendra Mohan. 1948. "The Contribution of Modern Indian Philosophy to World Philosophy." *Philosophical Review* 57, no. 6: 550–572.

Davis, Bret. 2019. "Knowing Limits: Toward a Versatile Perspectivism with Nietzsche, Heidegger, Zhuangzi and Zen." *Research in Phenomenology* 49: 301–334.

Doniger, Wendy O'Flaherty. 1984. *Dreams, Illusion, and Other Realities*. Chicago: University of Chicago Press.

Dreyfus, Hubert L., and Charles Taylor. 2015. *Retrieving Realism*. Cambridge, MA: Harvard University Press.

Eliot, T. S. [1919] 2001. "Tradition and the Individual Talent." In *The Waste Land and Other Writings*, 99–108. New York: Random House.

Emerson, Ralph Waldo. 2000. "The Over-soul." In *The Essential Writings of Ralph Waldo Emerson*, edited by Brooks Atkinson, 236–251. New York: Modern Library.

Eugeni, Ruggero. 2012. "First Person Shot: New Forms of Subjectivity Between Cinema and Intermedia Networks." *Anàlisi Monogràfic* 2–3: 19–31.

Fassbinder, Rainer Werner (dir.). 1973. *World on a Wire*. Criterion Collection [2012].

Frege, Gottlob. 1980. "On Sense and Meaning." In *Translations from the Philosophical Writings of Gottlob Frege*, edited by Peter Geach and Max Black, 157–177. Oxford: Basil Blackwell.

Galouye, Daniel F. 1999. *Simulacron-3*. Rockville, MD: Phoenix Pick.

Ganeri, Jonardon. 2017. "Freedom in Thinking: Intellectual Decolonisation and the Immersive Cosmopolitanism of K. C. Bhattacharyya." In *The Oxford Handbook of Indian Philosophy*, edited by Jonardon Ganeri, 718–736. Oxford: Oxford University Press.

Ganeri, Jonardon. 2018. "Illusions of Immortality." In *Imaginations of Death and the Beyond in India and Europe*, edited by Günter Blamberger and Sudhir Kakar, 35–45. Singapore: Springer Singapore.

Ganeri, Jonardon. 2019. "Epistemic Pluralism: From Systems to Stances." *Journal of the American Philosophical Association* 5, no. 1: 1–21.

Ganeri, Jonardon. 2021. *Virtual Subjects, Fugitive Selves: Fernando Pessoa and His Philosophy*. Oxford: Oxford University Press.

Ganeri, Jonardon. 2022. "Cosmic Consciousness." *The Monist* 105, no. 1: 43–57.

Ganeri, Jonardon. 2024. "Is It Possible to Imagine Being No-One?" *Journal of Consciousness Studies*, special issue titled *Is Subjectless Consciousness Possible?* Edited by Christian Coseru.

Gaultier, Jules de. 1910. *De Kant à Nietzsche*. Paris: Mercure de France. [Translated by G. M. Spring as *From Kant to Nietzsche* (New York: Philosophical Library, 1961). For Pessoa's copy, see CSP, http://bibliotecaparticular.casafernandopessoa.pt/1-52.]

Goff, Philip. 2017. *Consciousness and Fundamental Reality*. Oxford: Oxford University Press.

Hayashi, Keijin. 2001. "The Term 'True Dream' (*Satya-svapna*) in the Buddhist Epistemological Tradition." *Journal of Indian Philosophy* 29, nos. 5–6: 559–574.

Hazlitt, William. 1818. *Lectures on the English Poets: Delivered at the Surrey Institution*. Philadelphia: Thomas Dobson and Son.

Heidegger, Martin. 1996. *Being and Time*. Translated by Joan Stambaugh. Albany: State University of New York Press.

Henry, Victor. 1904. *Les Littératures de l'Inde: sanscrit, pâli, prâcrit*. Paris: Hachette. [For Pessoa's annotation, see CSP, http://bibliotecaparticular.casafernandopessoa.pt/8-250/2/8-250_master/8-250_PDF/8-250_0001_1-282_t24-C-R0150.pdf.]

Horner, I. B., trans. 1963. *Milinda's Questions*. Bristol: Pali Text Society.
James, William. 1890. *Principles of Psychology*. New York: Henry Holt.
James, William. 1902. *The Varieties of Religious Experience: A Study in Human Nature*. New York: Modern Library.
James, William. [1909] 2007. "The Confidences of a Psychical Researcher." In *William James: Essays and Lectures*, edited by Richard Kamber, 143–157. London: Routledge.
Jaynes, Julien. 1976. *The Origin of Consciousness in the Breakdown of the Bicameral Mind*. New York: Houghton Mifflin.
Johnston, Mark. 2010. *Surviving Death*. Princeton, NJ: Princeton University Press.
Keats, John. 2002. *Selected Letters of John Keats*. Cambridge, MA: Harvard University Press.
Kind, Amy, and Peter Kung. 2016. "Introduction." In *Knowledge Through Imagination*, edited by Amy Kind and Peter Kung, 1–38. Oxford: Oxford University Press.
Landy, Joshua. 2018. "To Thine Own Selves Be True-ish." In *Shakespeare's Hamlet: Philosophical Perspectives*, edited by Tzachi Zamir, 154–187. New York: Oxford University Press.
Langbaum, Robert Woodrow. 1977. *The Mysteries of Identity: A Theme in Modern Literature*. New York: Oxford University Press.
LdoD. Arquivo LdoD. https://ldod.uc.pt. [The sketches constituting *The Book of Disquiet*, cross-referenced against major editions.]
Lopes, Teresa Rita. 1990. *Pessoa por conhecer: textos para um novo mapa*. Lisbon: Estampa.
MacEwen, G. 1994. *Gwendolyn MacEwen: The Later Years*. Toronto: Exile Editions.
McLeod, Alexus. 2018. *Philosophy of the Ancient Maya: Lords of Time*. Lanham, MD: Lexington Books.
Mead, G. R. S. 1913. *Quests Old and New*. London: G. Bell and Sons. [For Pessoa's annotations, see CSP, http://bibliotecaparticular.casafernandopessoa.pt/1-105/1/1-105_item1/index.html?page=264.]
Miller, Henry. 1965. *Sexus: The Rosy Crucifixion*. New York: Grove Press.
Mitra, Vihari-Lala. (1891) 1999. *The Yoga-Vasishta Maharamayana of Valmiki*. Delhi: Low Price Publication. [Transcribed and edited by Thomas Palotas here: https://www.scribd.com/lists/2493058/Yoga-Vasishtha-Mitra-translation.]
MU = *Mokṣopāya*. [Susanne Krause-Stinner, ed., *Das erste und zweite Buch: Vairāgyaprakaraṇa; Mumukṣuvyavahāraprakaraṇa* (Wiesbaden: Harrassowitz, 2011. Jürgen Hanneder et al., eds., *Das dritte Buch: Utpattiprakaraṇa* (Wiesbaden: Harrassowitz, 2011). Susanne Krause-Stinner and Peter Stephan, eds., *Das vierte Buch: Sthitiprakaraṇa* (Wiesbaden: Harrassowitz, 2012). Susanne Krause-Stinner and Peter Stephan, eds., *Das*

fünfte Buch: Upaśāntiprakaraṇa (Wiesbaden: Harrassowitz, 2013). Susanne Krause-Stinner and Peter Stephan, eds., *Das Sechste Buch: Nirvāṇaprakaraṇa. Teil 1: 1–119* (Wiesbaden: Harrassowitz, 2018). Susanne Krause-Stinner and Anett Krause, eds., *Das Sechste Buch: Nirvāṇaprakaraṇa, Teil 2: 120–252* (Wiesbaden: Harrassowitz, 2019). This Sanskrit edition is available online at http://gretil.sub.uni-goettingen.de. A complete translation into English, by Vihari-Lala Mitra, was published in four volumes in 1891 (Mitra [1891] 1999), and a translation of select stanzas was published by Venkatesananda in 1984. An abridgement known as the *Laghu-yogavāviṣṭha* was translated into Persian at the Mughal court (Nair 2020).]

Morisson, Robert. *Nietzsche and Buddhism: A Study in Nihilism and Ironic Affinities*. Oxford: Oxford Unviersity Press, 1999.

Mota, Pedro da. 2016. "A Caminho do Oriente: apontamentos de Pessoa sobre Teosofia e espiritualidades da Índia." *Pessoa Plural* 10: 230–251.

Mukerji, A. C. 1938. *The Nature of Self*. Allahabad: The Indian Press.

Nair, Shankar. 2020. *Translating Wisdom: Hindu-Muslim Intellectual Interactions in Early Modern South Asia*. Berkeley: University of California Press.

Nanay, Bence. 2018. "Threefoldness." *Philosophical Studies* 175, no. 1: 163–182.

Nanay, Bence. 2019. *Aesthetics: A Very Short Introduction*. Oxford: Oxford University Press.

Nietzsche, Friedrich. 1980. *Sämtliche Werke. Kritische Studienausgabe in 15 Bänden*, edited by Giorgio Colli and Mazzino Montinari. Munich: De Gruyter.

Novillo-Corvalán, Patricia. 2020. "Borges's Shakespeare." In *Jorge Luis Borges in Context*, edited by Robin Fiddian, 149–157. Cambridge: Cambridge University Press.

Olivelle, Patrick. 1998. *The Early Upaniṣads*. Oxford: Oxford University Press.

Pachori, Satya S. 1996. "John Keats and Zen Buddhism: An Eastern Perspective." *South Asian Review* 20: 12–20.

Parfit, Derek. 1984. *Reasons and Persons*. Oxford: Clarendon Press.

Pater, Walter. 1878. "The Child in the House: An Imaginary Portrait." *Macmillan's Magazine*, August.

Perry, J. 1979. "The Problem of the Essential Indexical." *Noûs* 13, no. 1: 3–21.

Pessoa, Fernando. 1966. *Páginas íntimas e de auto-interpretação*. Edited by Georg Rudolf Lind e Jacinto do Prado Coelho. Lisbon: Ática.

Pessoa, Fernando. 1973. *Nova poesias inéditas*. Vol. 10 of *Obras completas de Fernando Pessoa*. Collected and edited with notes by Maria do Rosário Marques Sabino and Adelaide Maria Monteiro Sereno. Lisbon: Ática.

Pessoa, Fernando. 1985. *Fernando Pessoa e a filosofia hermética—fragmentos do espólio*. Edited by Y. K. Centeno. Lisbon: Presença.

Pessoa, Fernando. 1998. *Fernando Pessoa & Co.: Selected Poems*. Edited and translated by Richard Zenith. New York: Grove Press.

Pessoa, Fernando. 2001. *The Selected Prose of Fernando Pessoa*. Edited and translated by Richard Zenith. New York: Grove Press.

Pessoa, Fernando. 2002. *The Book of Disquiet*. Edited and translated by Richard Zenith. New York: Penguin. [First published in Portuguese as *Livro do Desassossego* (Lisbon: Assírio & Alvim, 1998).]

Pessoa, Fernando. 2002b. *Obras de António Mora*. Edited by Luis Filipe B. Teixeira. Imprensa Nacional-Casa da Moeda.

Pessoa, Fernando. 2006. *A Little Larger than the Entire Universe: Selected Poems*. Edited and translated by Richard Zenith. New York: Penguin.

Pessoa, Fernando. 2012. *Philosophical Essays: A Critical Edition*. Edited and translated by Nuno Ribeiro. New York: Contra Mundum Press.

Pessoa, Fernando. 2014. *The Transformation Book*. Edited and translated by Nuno Ribeiro. New York: Contra Mundum Press.

Pizzaro, Jerónimo, Patricio Ferrari, and Antonio Cardiello. 2011. "Os orientes de Fernando Pessoa." *Cultura Entre Culturas* 3: 148–185.

Proust, Marcel. 1982. *Remembrance of Things Past*. Translated by C. K. Scott Moncrieff and Terence Kilmartin. New York: Random House.

Radhakrishnan, Sarvepalli. 1936. *The World's Unborn Soul*. Oxford: Clarendon Press.

Rajasekharaiah, T. R. 1970. *The Roots of Whitman's Grass*. Rutherford, NJ: Fairleigh Dickinson University Press.

Raychaudhuri, Tapan. 1988. *Europe Reconsidered: Perceptions of the West in Nineteenth Century Bengal*. New Delhi: Oxford University Press.

Recanati, François. 2007. *Perspectival Thought: A Plea for (Moderate) Relativism*. Oxford: Oxford University Press.

Riccardi, Mattia. 2012. "António Mora and German Philosophy: Between Kant and Nietzsche." In *Pessoa in an Intertextual Web: Influence and Innovation*, edited by David Frier, 32–45. London: Legenda.

Ryan, Bartholomew. 2024. *Fernando Pessoa*. London: Reaktion Books.

Ryan, Bartholomew, Giovanbattista Tusa, and António Cardiello, eds. 2021. *Fernando Pessoa and Philosophy: Countless Lives Inhabit Us*. Lanham, MD: Rowman & Littlefield.

Schaffer, Jonathan. 2010. "Monism: The Priority of the Whole." *Philosophical Review* 119: 31–76.

Scheffler, Samuel. 2013. *Death and the After-life*. Edited by Niko Kodolny. Oxford: Oxford University Press.

Shani, Itay, and Keppler, Joachim. 2018. "Beyond Combination: How Cosmic Consciousness Grounds Ordinary Experience." *Journal of the American Philosophical Association* 4, no. 3: 390–410.

Shaw, George Bernard. 1931. "Credentials." In Frank Harris, *Bernard Shaw: An Unauthorised Biography Based on First-Hand Information with a Postscript by Mr Shaw*. London: Victor Gollancz, 1931.

Slaje, Walter. 2020. "Vasiṣṭha the Void: Inquiries into the Authorship of the *Mokṣopāya*." *Zeitschrift für Indologie und Südasienstudien* 37: 168–204.

Smith, John D. 2009. *The Mahābhārata*. New Delhi: Penguin.

Srivastava, K. G. 2002. *Bhagavad Gītā and the English Romantic Movement*. New Delhi: Macmillan India.

Strawson, Galen. 1989. "Red and 'Red.'" *Synthese* 78, no. 2: 193–232.

Strawson, Galen. 1999. "The Self and the SESMET." *Journal of Consciousness Studies* 6: 99–135.

Thompson, Evan. 2014. *Waking, Dreaming, Being: New Light on the Self and Consciousness from Neuroscience, Meditation and Philosophy*. New York: Columbia University Press.

Tulving, Envel. 1985. "Memory and Consciousness." *Canadian Psychology/Psychologie Canadienne* 26, no. 1: 1–12.

Tulving, Envel. 1993. "Varieties of Consciousness and Levels of Awareness in Memory." In *Attention: Selection, Awareness, and Control. A Tribute to Donald Broadbent*, edited by A. Baddeley and L. Weiskrantz, 283–299. Oxford: Oxford University Press, 1993.

Tulving, Envel. 2005. "Episodic Memory and Autonoesis: Uniquely Human?" In *The Missing Link in Cognition: Origins of Self-Reflective Consciousness*, edited by Herbert S. Terrace and Janet Metcalfe, 3–56. Oxford: Oxford University Press.

Valberg, Jerome J. 2007. *Dream, Death, and the Self*. Princeton, NJ: Princeton University Press.

Vendler, Zeno. 1979. "Vicarious Experience." *Revue de Métaphysique et de Morale* 84, no. 2: 161–173.

Vendler, Zeno. 1984. *The Matter of Minds*. Oxford: Clarendon Press.

Venkatesananda, Swami. 1984. *The Concise Yoga Vāsiṣṭha*. Albany: State University of New York Press.

Vivekananda, Swami. 1972. *The Complete Works of Swami Vivekananda*, vol. 7. Kolkata: Advaita Ashrama.

Walton, Kendall L. 1990. *Mimesis as Make-Believe: On the Foundations of the Representational Arts*. Cambridge, MA: Harvard University Press.

Weil, Simone. 1970. *First and Last Notebooks*. Translated by Richard Rees. London: Oxford University Press.

Wheeler, M. A., D. T. Stuss, and E. Tulving. 1997. "Toward a Theory of Episodic Memory: The Frontal Lobes and Autonoetic Consciousness." *Psychological Bulletin* 121, no. 3: 331–335.

Wiesing, Lambert. 2010. *Artificial Presence: Philosophical Studies in Image Theory*. Stanford, CA: Stanford University Press.

Williams, Bernard. 1973. *Problems of the Self: Philosophical Papers 1956–1972*. Cambridge: Cambridge University Press.

Williams, Bernard. 2002. *Truth and Truthfulness: An Essay in Genealogy*. Princeton, NJ: Princeton University Press.

Wollheim, Richard. 1980. "Seeing-as, Seeing-in, and Pictorial Representation." In *Art and Its Objects*, 2nd ed., 137–151. Cambridge: Cambridge University Press.

Wollheim, Richard. 1984. *The Thread of Life*. Cambridge, Mass: Harvard University Press.

Wujastyk, Dominik. 2021. "Sad News." *Indology* (listserv), posted May 15, 2021. https://www.mail-archive.com/indology@list.indology.info/msg00098.html.

Zavatta, Benedetta. 2021. "Pessoa and American Transcendentalism." In *Fernando Pessoa and Philosophy: Countless Lives Inhabit Us*, edited by Bartholomew Ryan, Giovanbattista Tusa, and António Cardiello, 141–164. Lanham, MD: Rowman & Littlefield.

Zenith, Richard. 2021. *Pessoa: A Biography*. New York: Liveright.

Index

absurd, the, 70–2
acting, 2, 14–5, 31, 50–1, 86, 89, 97, 104. *See also* theatre
admiration, 16–8, 22–3, 38, 55, 57, 63
Advaita Vedānta, 116, 122–3, 132, 141, 144. *See also* Śaṅkara
aesthetics and aesthetic experience, 18, 105, 113–5
Alford, Lucy, 7, 22
Amiel, Henri-Frédéric, 5–6
artefact mind. *See* heteronym
Arunachalam, Ponnambalam, 126
astonishment, 16–8, 23, 38, 55, 57, 63
attention, 7, 17, 25, 72, 83, 89, 92
  poetic, 20–2, 38, 55, 106
  self-, 43
  singly focused (*eka-dhyāna*), 60
  twofold, 19
avatāra, 2
  defined, 49
  vs. avatar, 5, 48–52

Baldaya, Raphael (Pessoa's heteronym), 121
bearing, cognitive and affective, 14, 32
  defined, 1–2
  vs. mere reincarnation, 5, 33, 41, 48, 53
Besant, Annie, 118–121, 144
Bhagavad-gītā, the, 8, 50, 54, 61, 126, 130, 141, 145
Bhattacharyya, Krishnachandra, 111–2, 124
Borges, Jorge Luis, 14–5, 61
Buddhism, 53, 84, 113–4
  echoes in Pessoa, 30

Caeiro, Alberto (Pessoa's heteronym) 3, 8, 21, 23, 32–3, 36, 38, 41, 45, 77, 94–6, 101
  attending Caeiroesquely, 19, 37
  "The Keeper of Sheep," 30
Campos, Álvaro de (Pessoa's heteronym), 3, 8, 19, 21, 30, 32, 101
Carpenter, Edward, 125ff. 141, 144
Cartesian
  fantasy, 43, 54, 82
  Pessoa's anti- 64
Chakrabarti, Arindam, vii, 52, 128
Chalmers, David, 4, 47–9, 52–3, 81, 96. *See also* virtual realism
Christianity, 111, 114–5, 121
Coleridge, Samuel Taylor, 139–41, 145
cosmic consciousness, 103, 125ff.
cosmopsychism
  defined, 137
  heteronymic, 141–4
  impersonal version of, 139–40
  personal version of, 140

Dasgupta, Surendranath, 123–4

death, 58, 92, 119, 131
as deletion, 68 ff.
as sleep, 69
democracy, 129–31, 135, 141
depersonalization, 4–5, 64
defined, 31
Diderot, Denis, 20
double, the in literature, 25, 63, 102–3
dream, 54, 69, 72, 78, 82 ff., 91–3, 95–6, 98, 109
the body in a (*svapnāntika-śarīra*), 53–4
as a frame of heteronymy, 21, 24, 27, 41, 49, 60, 68, 77
highest stage of, defined, 4, 63–4
–man (*svapna-puruṣa*), 58–9
Pessoa's technical use of, defined, 33, 36, 43, 94
self-estrangement within, 26, 32, 51, 113
Zhuangzi's, 61
dreaming vs. waking experience, 89
Dreyfus, Hubert, 90

Eliot, T. S., 12
embodiment, 1, 11–12, 61, 105
immersion as, 33
virtual, 48–9, 52 (*see also* reincarnation)
Emerson, Ralph Waldo, 140–1, 145
emotions, 2, 46, 53, 55, 72, 134, 136
dramatized, 31, 51, 86, 105
as a mode of poetic attention, 22–3
self-conscious, 16
virtual, 42, 45
empathic coupling, 44–7, 77, 96

Fassbinder, Rainer Werner, 44
first-person
positional vs. indexical use of, 25, 28
shot, in film, 44–5
See also imagining: *de se*
Frege, Gottlob, 98–9

Galouye, Daniel, 42, 45–7, 96
Simulacron-3, 42ff. 55, 78, 82, 92
See also empathic coupling
Gandhi, Mahatma, 112, 130
Gaultier, Jules de, 115–6
Ghose, Aurobindo, 122

Harivaṃśa, the, 50–1
Hazlitt, William, 13–4, 17, 140
Henry, Victor, 115
heteronym, 6, 19, 26, 31, 43, 53, 91, 93, 96
defined, 3–4, 142
individuals as *brahman*'s, 125ff.
interactions between, 32
life as a chain of, 55–63, 77
lived in parallel, 63–73
medium of, 103
reality of, 83, 94
vs. pseudonym, 50, 56–7, 142
heteronymy, 89
and acting, 50–1, 104
frame of, 21, 25, 27, 41, 53
as intersubjective transference, 60
in Maya Philosophy, 68
in *Simulacron-3*, 42 ff., 55
use of a name twice over, and, 94ff.
vs. mere incarnation, 48–9
Hinduism, 113, 116, 141
horizon, experiential, 27–8, 32

idealism, 83, 90, 93, 116, 120, 122–4
identity
"is," of, 37, 119
national, 117
necessity of, 27–8, 99
personal, 2, 6, 11–12, 14, 30, 42, 58, 61, 63, 66–8, 104, 131, 133, 142
trans-simulation object, 81–5

illusion, 93, 100, 131
art as, 93
māyā as (see *māyā*)
simulations as, 81–5
world as (*see* Indian ideal, the)
imaginary portraits, 21
imagination, 1–2, 12, 14, 17, 23, 28, 31, 94, 101–2, 105, 109, 128, 145
creative, 16, 83–4
as generator of virtual realities, 5, 21, 33
intersubjective transference in, 60
as mode of poetic attention, 22
imagining, 28, 83–4, 87–9
de se, 1–4, 31, 32ff., 62, 64
heteronymic, 37
quasi-de se, 36
seeing oneself, 21, 100–3
immersion, 1, 4–5, 12, 33, 48, 51–4, 60, 81, 89, 92, 96–7, 101–2
immersive centrality vs. immersive for-me-ness, 7, 38
Pessoa as the poet of, 7, 16
positionality as, 25–9, 41, 45
immortality, 56–8, 68–71, 136
imperialism, internal logic of, 109–13, 121–2
and cultural subjection, 112
"Indian ideal", the, 113ff.
intersectionism, 21, 25, 68, 91, 98

James, William, 88, 125–6, 137–40
Jaynes, Julian, 71
Johnston, Mark, 28–32, 61

Keats, John, 11ff. 136, 140
kṛtrima, 51–2. *See* reality: artificial

life, as an intelude, 70–2

Mahābhārata, the
Draupadī's polyandry, 64–6
Indra's heteronymy, 66
māyā, 50, 99, 115–6, 123–4
as artistic power, 52, 82
Maya philosophy, 66–8
k'ex 'substitution', 67
Mead, George, 115
memory, 22, 34, 90
asymmetry assumption, 78, 81, 92
episodic, 87–8
quasi-, 36
Miller, Henry, 54
misidentification, immunity of error due to, 100, 102
modernism, crisis of, 20
Mokṣopāya, the (aka *Yogavāsiṣṭha*), 2, 8, 75ff., 103–4, 127–8
Story of a Hundred Rudras, 55ff. 78, 82, 95
Story of Lavaṇa, 53, 78ff., 98–100, 105
Story of Second Līlā, 52, 78, 94ff.
monism, 123
priority vs. existence, 122, 137, 141
psychological, 132, 144
Śaṅkara's (*see* Śaṅkara)
Mora, António (Pessoa's heteronym), 113, 115
morality, 20, 29, 47, 50, 65, 82, 114
Mukerji, Anukulchandra, 122–3

Nāgārjuna, 63
Nagel, Thomas, 69
Nanay, Bence, 18, 97
Navya-nyāya, 117
Nietzsche, Friedrich, 20, 114, 116, 124

orthonym, 8, 46, 89, 96, 103

Parfit, Derek, 63
Perry, John, 100
Pessoa, Fernando
Autopsychography, 31, 105
Countless Lives Inhabit Us, 31

Pessoa, Fernando (*cont.*)
and India, 109ff.
I'm a Fugitive, 104–5
In the Forest of Estrangement, 4, 21, 24, 38, 51, 66, 78, 91
Notes for the Memory of My Master Caeiro, 5, 21, 32, 94, 96
and the occult, 114, 120–1
as poet-scientist, 5–6, 43
Time's Passage, 3
The Mariner, 91–2
The Book of Disquiet, 3–4, 6, 17–18, 24–5, 29–30, 43, 63–4, 68–73, 77, 85, 94, 109, 142–3
pictures, 73, 94–7
pluralism, 8, 22, 101, 120, 135, 137
"Be plural like the universe!," 3, 11, 16–8, 55, 90, 125, 140
epistemic, 90, 93
heteronymic, 54, 55
metaphysical, 5, 20, 77, 86
pluralization
by self-estrangement vs. by living a life in parallel, 4, 25–6
poetry
defined, 16–19, 38
double transitivity of, 22
poet's creed, the, 11ff.
polytheism, 114
Prajñākaragupta, 54
Protean persons, 13–4, 61
Proust, Marcel, 20

Queiroz, Ofélia, 109

Radhakrishnan, Sarvepalli, 124, 132–5, 144
Ramaswami (Carpenter's guru) 137–8, 132, 141
Reality++, 5, 77ff.
reality, 23, 25, 70, 82–3, 86, 96, 103, 122, 137
absolute, 115, 123ff.
artificial, 24, 33, 51–2, 97
levels vs. domains, 77, 85, 87–8, 98
virtual, 3, 7, 24, 31, 33, 41, 45, 47–9, 52–3, 86, 97
ways of interrogating, 90, 100
Recanati, François, 33, 36, 101–2
reincarnation, 2, 32, 54, 67
Reis, Ricardo (Pessoa's heteronym) 3, 8, 19
Ryan, Bartholomew, 2

Śaṅkara, 116–7, 119, 122, 141, 144
self
conceptions of, 4, 7, 11–12, 18, 27–8, 30, 34–7, 41, 51, 72–3, 78, 96, 104–5, 111, 118–9, 122–3, 128–31, 133–4, 141–3
fragmentation of, 20–1
self-awareness, 17, 42–3, 131
forumnal vs heteronymic, 103–4
self-estrangement, 4–5, 24ff., 41, 89
self-knowledge, 5, 93
Shakespeare, William, 5, 13ff., 17, 61, 140
Hamlet, 5, 15, 31
Shaw, George Bernard, 15
simulation, 5, 21, 31–3, 42–55, 77–8, 80–6, 90, 96–8, 101, 142, 145
entrance, immersion and exit phases
hypothesis, 42
poems as, 7, 41
Strawson, Galen, 30
subjectivity, 7, 17, 69, 72, 111, 131, 133

Taylor, Charles, 90
The Makropulos Case, 55ff.
theatre
as a metaphor, 14, 50, 71, 89, 97, 104
See also acting
Theosophy, 118, 120–2, 144

Thompson, Evan, 51
trans-simulation object identity, hypothesis of, 81–3
Tulving, Envel, 87–8

Upaniṣads, the, 91, 93, 116–21, 134, 141, 143–4

Valberg, Jeremy, 26–8, 32–3, 45, 53, 84–5, 96, 98
Vasiṣṭha, 8, 60–1, 82ff., 103
Vendler, Zeno, 1, 33, 35, 60, 101–2, 104
virtual realism, 81, 83, 96–7
virtual reality environment, 32–3, 81
virtual self. *See* heteronym
Vivekananda, Swami, 117

Walton, Kendall, 33, 35–6, 83–4
what vs. how, 7, 18–9, 21, 45, 100
Whitman, Walt, 8, 22, 31, 130, 132, 136
Wiesing, Lambert, 97
Williams, Bernard, 20, 33–6, 56–7, 62
Wollheim, Richard, 6, 19, 62–3, 97

Yeats, W. B., 20

Zen, 12–3, 15
Zenith, Richard, 2, 4, 6–7, 26, 30–1, 55, 66, 68, 91, 130
Zhuangzi, the, 61, 92